novum premium

PHAN MINH THONG

Overcoming Business Journeys

A collection of stories and separate notes

novum premium

www.novum-publishing.co.uk

All rights of distribution, including via film, radio, and television, photomechanical reproduction, audio storage media, electronic data storage media, and the reprinting of portions of text, are reserved.

Printed in the European Union on environmentally friendly, chlorine- and acid-free paper.

© 2023 novum publishing

ISBN 978-3-99130-251-3
Editing: Chris Beale
Cover photo:
Pishit Kamsink I Dreamstime.com
Cover design, layout & typesetting: novum publishing
Author's photo: Phan Minh Thong

www.novum-publishing.co.uk

CONTENTS

Copyright	7
Author's Words	8
Acknowledgements	9
Business Portrait during Covid	10
Sad Story	18
Broken Wings	24
Doing Business during Covid	28
Fierce Market	31
End-of-Year Reflection 1	34
Debt Collecting	39
Narrowly Escaping Fraud	46
Difficulty in doing Business (*Narrowly Escaping Fraud 2*)	57
Unique Businesses	62
End-of-Year Reflection 2	66
Business Lawsuit	70
Happy Life	76
Association	77
Business Trip	84
Vietnamese Women *Dedicated to Vietnamese Women*	89
I go retailing	96
An American Trip	98
Price of Art	107
Business Culture	111
Why doesn't Vietnamese Coffee have a Global Brand yet?	114

Happy Thoughts during Covid 118
A pungent Year – a bitter-sweet Year 121
365 Days of Connection 127
End-of-Year Reflection 3 131
Authentic CEOs 139
Love of Arts 146

COPYRIGHT

Artwork: Overcoming Business Journeys

Author: Phan Minh Thong

Copyright of this work belongs to the author. No part of this work may be reproduced or transmitted in any form, by any means, whether electronic, print, sound recording or any information retrieval and storage system, without the prior written consent of the author.

PHAN MINH THONG

AUTHOR'S WORDS

I wrote *Overcoming Business Journeys* in four years, with most of the writing completed during the time of Covid-19. Whenever I heard a good, inspirational story, or an experience of success or failure, I would write it down. I usually write in a narrative style in order to convey a story, an event, or a certain moment. Yet, there were times when I thought: "Why shouldn't I just create and expand the stories and add more characters? Life is already a great story with so many unique characters. A story with characters and details would be more interesting. Furthermore, when a story is written and published, it develops an independent life of its own, compared to articles." Therefore, I was happy with that discovery and have written more different stories since.

Writing is a challenge for me. Even so, I released my second publication containing many articles accessible to the public. In my first publication, *Unlimited Creativity in Business* (2017), there was praise as well as criticism. Yet, in the end, more than 13,000 copies were sold, enough to cover all the publication costs. Four years after publication, I continued to sell the book, and many people still send us touching words, sharing such useful stories. With these lessons from the readers, I am even more inspired. Whenever I find a good story, I choose to keep on writing in a way for people to experience it. Perhaps that is exactly the motivation for my second publication: *Overcoming Business Journeys*.

With real stories and experiences from the realm of business, I hope every reader will benefit from reading it. Notwithstanding both praise and criticism, I look forward to listening to both in order to learn, experience and grow even more.

I am grateful that you have picked this book up, opened it, and read it through!

ACKNOWLEDGEMENTS

Special thanks to my company assistants Minh Trang, Camelia and my son Minh Phuc for their enthusiasm in helping with the Vietnamese-English translation. This publication would not be possible without their dedicated effort and passion. Lastly, I am grateful to my son Minh Quang for supporting me in finalizing this project.

BUSINESS PORTRAIT DURING COVID

Throughout 2020, the entire world was reeling under Covid. From Europe, then the US: daily news about Covid, daily images of sick people in the hospitals, howling ambulances. Talking to clients, we could hear the panic in their voices. After clients had spent so much time at home, we could observe the pain in their faces. Fortunately, at that time, Vietnam had not been seriously affected. But on the business side, things were not that easy.

"Mr. Quang, the price of peppercorn has become too high and continues to rise, almost doubling compared to the same period last year!" the Purchasing Director, Viet Anh, called to say.

"Really? How could the price increase continuously under Covid? Send me the report from the last few months."

"Peppercorn prices have been increasing continuously for nearly two months, but just now is the sharpest rise. Almost double compared to 2019. Is the supply limited? How should we decide?" Viet Anh asked.

"I did anticipate issues with the supply, but did not expect the speculators to seize this opportunity to push the price up that badly. Just buy enough goods for the pending signed contracts," I replied.

"We lose a lot with the signed contracts ... What then, Mr. Quang?" the sales manager, Lee, asked me at the meeting.

"We still have to buy it, Lee. We still have to deliver cargo to our buyers even with a loss, but the price will increase immediately. Viet Anh, make the plan to buy twice as much for me."

when the price goes up, the suppliers will
ock and won't sell. It's the same every year.
ffer a huge loss if they sell, and won't buy at

"I know. Try to buy enough and then double the quantity for me."

The price of agricultural products had risen, but coffee prices hadn't. Coffee growers and exporters were devastated! Lee mentioned she was also working with the Operation Department regarding freight charges.

"The freight charge went up so much, while our sale contracts are fixed, as the freight charge goes up daily, I can see terrible losses. What should we do?" Lee said.

"What is the reason for this increase in freight rate?" Mr. Quang asked.

"Due to the severe pandemic in many countries, many container yards do not have enough workers and arriving ships only clog up more containers. There are no empty containers at the ports with no one to move them. Shipping companies picked up on that and pushed the freight rates up, piling up even more challenges for companies. Now, companies are in an even more difficult situation, as we cannot get empty containers at a low rate as agreed, the shipping company has canceled all their prior commitments!", Lee said.

"Why would they do that? They just canceled all of their commitments?"

"Yes," Lee replied.

"In my opinion, just let me keep trying to persuade the shipping company. In the past, we treated them kindly and generously, so they shouldn't treat us so badly," said Rose, the Operation Director.

We kept spinning like pinwheels. Customers were affected by the Covid pandemic, so money was short. It was also difficult to gain payment. Many Europe companies had to close due to the pandemic, without revenue. And now, with this flood of new difficulties, employees were asking, "What should we do now? What can we do?"

Many people thought the crisis would only last a few months before commodity prices returned to normal, and the same for freight rates. But no! This was just the beginning.

The phone rang. "Mr. Quang, did you know that the Lien Nga warehouse, which worked with us, just went bankrupt? The goods they delivered were quite decent."

"What happened?"

"The warehouse owners thought the coffee price would remain stable for years, that it would probably be okay for them to take the coffee from the people and send to the customers. Now that the price of coffee has gone up and there is no money to pay people, they've run away, no one can contact them!"

Hien, the director of the coffee factory called. "Mr. Quang, I just heard from the market that JF Coffee Company has gone bankrupt. And at Sede Company, the director just took all documents regarding the goods and ran away."

"I've just been informed that the world's second largest coffee trading company, Amarex, has just declared bankruptcy, and is being sold to a competitor for one Euro. Once valued at 30 billion euros, this company had 30 offices worldwide! The coffee business is very tough," I said.

There are more and more warehouses, factories, companies … people who lack capital, defaulted people and people without hedge facilities.

"Lee, why won't the customers open an LC[1] for us to deliver?" I asked.

"I've been trying to persuade them for a month, even though they signed the contract. Now they don't have money and are unable to sell goods for cash while the bank is tightening and reducing the credit limit. It's too hard, the customers don't know what to do. Then what about our goods? They are already available. The quality will be a problem."

"You must find a way to sell it to someone else," I instructed.

During 2020, the business rhythm continued to be similarly stressful, with many tragic bankruptcy stories due to high

---

1 LC: Letter of credit payment guarantee for import and export of goods.

peppercorn prices. Taking people's goods and having no money to pay, the companies that sold cargo before buying in at a high price eventually went bankrupt. For the coffee industry, many warehouses went bankrupt because the price of coffee did not rise as expected. Instead of going up, the price went down.

The entire world hoped for a vaccine, and the media provided the news regarding a vaccine. At the end of the year, news about a vaccine being endorsed and circulated in the US and Europe allowed everyone to rekindle business activities again. But for Vietnam, the pandemic had just begun.

2021

During a brief meeting, An, the Human Resources Administration Director said, "Mr. Quang, I hear the pandemic is going to be more intense, and the city government will make things more difficult; perhaps it will even completely lock down. This time they will probably be stricter than before."

"Yes, I also think the same from reading the newspaper, but I think as we are in the export business of agricultural products and we also do business in essential domestic goods, the government will still allow us to operate partially. For countries around the world, when pandemics occur, they still allow trade in essential goods or the export of agricultural products. However, we must strictly adhere to safety and distance."

"We conclude many contracts and borrow a lot from the bank in order to export, so we have to keep those companies running that gain enough money for us to pay the bank. And we always have to maintain our reputation with suppliers and banks so that doing business in the future will be easier," Viet, the CFO[2], said.

---

2 CFO: Chief Financial Officer.

"That's right, I think so. Besides, over 300 people are in the system, including officials, workers, and management staff. It would be hard for most people if we were not working. Too many people in their families have already lost their jobs. It would be too difficult for companies and factories to stop now. How could they live?" An, the HR Director said.

We had to be determined to find a way of surviving. We also believed that exports, port operations and essential businesses could still operate as long as hygiene safety was maintained. And, specifically, to find a vaccine source for all employees.

Many things happened: Covid spread worldwide, customers were exhausted financially, people were hurting, and there were mental health problems everywhere. Once Covid was raging violently in Vietnam, it caused deep desperation in production and business activities.

An entered my office and said, "Mr. Quang, we should arrange accommodation for people to stay in the office; I think it's likely that they won't let us go out on the street. And I will make some contacts to have a travel permit issued by the Department of Industry and Trade."

"Well, luckily, we provide food in our restaurant at the company … and bedrooms, so I don't suppose it would be too difficult, right?"

"I think so too. Let me do it."

And we did, quickly and efficiently. There is always an opportunity to keep the connection between people and business unbroken. We were in the business of essential goods, and when things became difficult, we considered quitting. What else can I say? But these were essential services for the world economy: exporting agricultural products from millions of farmers, creating revenue for the whole industry. It was also necessary to repay loans, which could not be stopped. We deployed quickly, but encountered many difficulties that we didn't anticipate.

"Mr. Quang, I never imagined being at home would cause so much stress. Mental health concerns and stress make me unable to predict anything. Ms. Huong, the Secretary, wants to go back to her hometown because she's afraid of the pandemic …," said An.

"Why don't you try to convince her?"

"I did, but she cried and insisted on quitting … Why would she quit at a difficult time like this? Quitting now would make things difficult for the Administration Department. Even if we refuse to allow her to quit, she'll still do it anyway. Two days later, Lynda also sent her resignation. Her family kept calling her to stay home, and she finally had to quit. Nga was also crying in my office. Her husband and mother wouldn't let her come to work, and Nha also asked me to let her go."

"Nha, the one that was so cute?"

"Yes, that's her. She didn't want to quit, but her mother pushed her hard, and she was too afraid of the pandemic. Her mother kept calling and crying; she couldn't bear it …"

"But everyone is vaccinated. What if the pandemic lasts the whole year, like Europe and the US?" said Quang.

"They can't think of all that now, they're too scared. Who else will quit?" I asked myself.

When we were at the office, sleeping and eating also became a headache. The mattresses were too hard; the food was unsuitable; the challenge of cleaning things, especially the inability to go out, put most people under a lot of stress. Looking back one week, there was so much pain in people's faces. Looking back two weeks, I found myself having to be more patient. An inner voice told me something needed to be done to lift people's spirits and get through this difficult time.

I made a speech. I shared about companies in the services industry: hotels, airlines, housing, real estate, tourism companies that had to close … people losing their jobs with no income and business owners having to sell their houses and cars to pay debts. Many people ended up selling everything they had.

Millions of people were unemployed, and we were so lucky to be able to work and get our full salary. We could still meet and talk to each other and be able to talk with and meet our customers and suppliers. We were still able to feel angry or happy; we were still able to share ... We did everything I thought we could. Then, eventually, we went through each day like that.

"Is today Saturday?" Mr. Phan of the Finance Department spoke out, making me feel very happy. At least working would distract us, and people wouldn't have any negative thoughts. A week went by very quickly.

We tried to get a travel permit because we were a rather large-scale export company. With just a minor change from the city, everyone could go home and then return to work, reducing the pressure on the restaurant's kitchen staff and the Administrative Department. At least we could still work. The factory was still operating despite of 40 percent reduction in capacity. We still had revenue, everyone was fully paid, and we still borrowed from and repaid the bank.

"Many customers have told me it was fortunate that Kphucsinh.vn was still active and delivering; without KPhucSinh now, they wouldn't know where to buy essential goods."

"Mr. Quang, I couldn't call KPhucSinh. Please help me, tell your employees to call me. I already ordered on the web." Just like that, we worked together on delivery. Actions like that helped us survive the pandemic.

Phuc Sinh Consumer Corporation kept going, while people at other companies were too scared and quit, or the other companies couldn't continue their business. We thought we couldn't pay everyone's salary if we quit then. Many people still needed to buy food, and they waited for us to provide delivery. We had to try, try harder. Going to work made us feel a lot of empathy during those four long months. We felt a desire to share food with others. Going to work relieved us from being inhibited at home. When we went to work, we often forgot all the difficulties and hearing, "Tomorrow is Saturday, huh, so fast?" That made me happy, and we felt that life was also brighter.

"Mr. Quang, today is the second anniversary of your management of Phuc Sinh Consumer Corporation. The business results in August are great; for the first time we have a good profit," said the chief accountant, entering my office. Really? Two years of performing the executive job are during two years of Covid, with many difficulties and challenges.

My company still pays the bank the interest for due-date debt, and the factories still ship the goods worldwide. One day, when I went to disburse, the person in charge of the bank said, "Today, I'm only disbursing for your company; all the other companies have already closed."

"Yes, we are still producing, paying off bank loans and even paying everyone a monthly salary, and as long as the business is still operating, we will still live," said Viet, the Finance Director.

The ambulances were still running, but there seemed to be fewer. Adjustments began, and economic recovery plans rekindled. And here: "Hey, confirm this lot of ten containers, book the empty containers, and make a loading plan for next week ..."

Covid during lockdown days, September 16, 2021.

SAD STORY

I called my mom when I decided to quit my job and start a new company.

"Mom, I quit my job at the company I was working for and opened a new company."

"So, why did you leave that company? The job was going well."

"They changed personnel, Mom, and I had to transfer my favorite product to someone else and I like doing this line of work so I quit my job and opened a company."

"I don't know much, but please take care!"

At 25, I didn't have many talents, but when I quit my job at my old company, I had some business relationships. I had US$3,000, so I rented a small office to operate out of. After a month, our office had four people about the same age as me. It must be said that at that time, the cost was quite low. Twenty years ago, the chief accountant's salary was US$120 per month, and an employee's salary was from US$80 to US$220.

We sat in a small office of about 17 square meters, with another room of 8 square meters for meeting with customers. The work ethic was low, so I had to put a lot of effort into motivating the staff.

Startups don't have much, but I had my health and willpower, and there was no backing down anyway.

"Mr. Minh, can I talk to you for a moment?" Duong, a forwarder and customs officer, who had only been working for a little over a month, asked me.

"Okay." Everyone else had already gone home, so it was just the two of us. "Yeah," I said, "stay here and talk."

"Mr. Minh, I am getting married soon, but neither family is rich ... Could you lend me money for the wedding?"

"Borrow money for the wedding? So, the marrying couple has no money?"

"No, we don't have any. Please lend me money; I will collect the lucky money and pay you back after I get married."

I also had just married. We lived in a small apartment of 47 square meters on the fifth floor of a building with no elevator, right next door to the company.

"Okay, tomorrow I will go to the bank to withdraw money to lend you."

In fact, I had no money. Just the US$3000 to set up the company. Fortunately, though, I had a credit limit at the bank, so I could withdraw money for loans.

I came home to talk to my wife. "Honey, at the office there is this young fellow, Duong. He wants to borrow money for his wedding."

"Why is he borrowing money for the wedding? He has only been working for the company for just over a month …"

"Yes, but I agreed."

As a startup, we worked like crazy. Even at 2 a.m., when American customers called, I would still answer the phone. I only slept a few hours a day.

Six months later, "Mr. Minh, can I talk to you for a moment?" Was there a problem? "I have something to ask you …," said Duong.

"Okay, come into the meeting room and let's talk."

"Mr. Minh, my wife and I want to buy a house. Can you lend us money?"

"Buy a house … You want to borrow money to buy a house?"

"Yes, we will pay you 2 million VND per month."

Thinking for no more than 60 seconds, I agreed. I lent Duong money to buy a house. I think I did all this money lending to people because I was young then, had an easy character, and made such quick and easy decisions. Later, I asked myself many times, would it have been so easy to lend him money if I was more mature? Would I have lent him money for his wedding when he only worked for me for over one month? Or would it have been easy to lend him money to buy a house?

And then I came home to talk to my wife. "Honey, Duong borrowed money to buy a house. Paying 2 million VND per month."

"God, a wedding loan and now a home loan?"

"I agree, but he has been working for me for six months and is doing well, so I decided to help him."

The office had grown tremendously, from four to over 30 people, and we also built two factories. Things developed, but finding the CEO (Executive Director) for the factory was not easy.

After many failed attempts, I called Duong. "Duong, I would like to talk to you. Do you want to be the factory Director? You've been working here in this small office for a long time now. If you stay here, it will be difficult for everyone after you to develop. Men should also move around a bit to gain experience. A factory Director would have their own car and a higher salary …"

After a few minutes, Duong replied, "I will go there, but with the condition that I have my friend Quan, who is head of the Assessment Department, accompany me."

"Oh, okay, no problem."

So, Duong went down to the factory to work as a director. The work was very good, the factory was successful, and the production was continuous.

Three years later ...

During a celebration party, we discussed success with our partners when I suddenly said, "Duong, the company will lend you 30 percent of the needed funds to buy a high-class apartment. What do you think?"

"That's great. I'll go back and talk to my wife, and we'll prepare the papers."

We spent the next five years developing steadily, but by the eighth year, things went south. I was informed that the director didn't work properly, and things were a mess.

Success was great, but winning all the time made people grow vulnerable. When something went wrong, people didn't deal with it well. When it happened continuously, people tried to hide it. In fact, I think I was guilty of many things, especially regarding supervision. Being the CEO of the Group means creating job opportunities for others, but at the same time, I have to observe closely. By observing and managing, there is less risk for me as well as others.

Incidentally, we had a new director position available in another company of ours, which had been established for just three years. One day I invited Duong over for a drink. After a few glasses, I said to him, "I need someone for the position of Director in Saigon. Can you go and work there?"

"Haven't you hired a CEO for this project already?"

"Not yet, and you would have a better salary!"

"I agree. I think there's nothing that I can't succeed at! By the way, could I ask the company to help provide confirmation for my relatives, so that I can send my children and wife to Australia? I would like for my children to study there." Duong said.

"So, you're settling down in Australia?"

"No, my wife is just taking our children to study there."

I got the detailed internal report from the factory, and I couldn't believe it!

"Are we really at a loss like this?" I asked.

"The warehouse must have overstated the data, sir!" Dung, the CFO, informed me. "I couldn't sleep all night; how could this be?"

"Tomorrow, organize a meeting with Duong for me," I told Dung.

"Yes," he said.

"How could you write 'peppercorn shells' in for such heavy peppercorn?" I asked Duong. "You say you're sorry, but the Company had to buy poor peppercorns, and the seller delivered bad quality. I'm at a loss! And you didn't tell me. Why would you and the chief accountant report and record large profits, divide the rewards, and pay large amounts of corporate income tax? Writing flat peppercorn into heavy peppercorn makes a difference of tens of billions!"

Duong was silent!

"What happened, Duong?"

He was still quiet ... "I'm sorry," he said quietly.

"Correct the records, and let me know the exact number of the losses," I told Dung, the CFO. "And reduce Duong's salary by 30 percent!"

I still couldn't find out the reason. Someone who had worked with me for 16 years ... To cheat all the books of accounts, overstate inventory and take big bonuses when the company had a loss? I treated him well. What was my mistake?

"Can't you see that you've made a big mistake?" My wife spoke up. "You give power to people simply on trust, but do not keep them in check. One day you will regret that!"

Humans are all the same; they are used to success, not failure.

If you monitor them closely, apart from the fact that you wouldn't lose money, you also wouldn't lose people. Businesses must have a strict monitoring system. The bigger it is, the more powerful the monitoring and control needs to be. You cannot only rely on trust.

A heavy atmosphere enveloped the entire system and factory, as Duong had worked there for a long time and was familiar with everyone. Most of the staff looked at me with pity, but some people defended Duong. There is a saying I've heard: "No matter how well you do, there will be critics, and no matter how much you do wrong, there will always be supporters."

After a few months, Duong left the company. He quit his job and moved to Australia to settle down. I later read a letter from Duong when he quit, saying that I had enticed him to Saigon to be the Director and let all the staff know about how he forged inventory figures, causing him to fail at the new company.

Looking back on the incident, I was deeply saddened. Sixteen years of work, and now the outcome is this? Didn't I know I was losing too much?

"Mr. Minh, I can't believe it! Mr. Duong is suing us." The Human Resources Director, Linh, rushed into my room.

"What's wrong?"

"He's suing us for not paying him as much as we did at his last company, when we paid the individuals who quit before 2009."

"But aren't they different companies?"

Five months later, Linh rushed into my room and exclaimed. "The court ruled that Duong has lost the case. He really has no shame at all!" I looked at Linh. I didn't feel happy at all, only pain!

"How can people be so horrible? To cause such a significant loss! And still try and sue us over US$ 500," Linh said, and then continued, "I have just received a letter from Duong, which he sent me from Australia. He wrote that he lived and worked at the Group all his youth, and now he feels only regret …"

Covid during lockdown days, September 10, 2021.

BROKEN WINGS

I still hope to receive Lynda's wedding invitation to see the joyful bride and groom marry. That is one of the beautiful things that, as a CEO, I think I have aided in creating. The joy, the American Dream ...

Sara pushed open the door. "David, I just talked to Lynda. The conversation was heartfelt, and I was quite surprised she thought that way!"

"How so?"

"She said she was very unhappy with the company, especially you, David. During the six months of the pandemic, being stuck in New York, taking care of the students, and how you didn't thank her. Plus, she had to work as a housekeeper with no compensation! Three years working with no salary increase and many other things ... The pandemic scares her ... she wants to quit. Does the company take care of her? If she got sick, who would be responsible for her? The company didn't take care of the vaccine for her ... she has to take care of everything herself ... and she doesn't want to work. If the company lets her work from home, she'll stay; otherwise, she will quit."

"God, why is it like that? Staying at home for only two weeks, and she's already turned into a different person! Two weeks ago, she was so happy and positive."

"I think maybe it's because of staying at home, the pandemic, the negative news ... and I think many people are stressed right now."

"Well, let's take it slow and hope everyone calms down by tomorrow."

"Yes, I think so too."

When Sara left the office, I sat alone, thinking, trying to connect the lines of thought somehow. How could that be? Every time we talk, I always say thanks to her. Maybe I didn't specifically thank her for the whole thing, perhaps what Lynda had hoped for. But three years without a raise? In fact, the company did not do very well the last three years, making just enough to cover and pay off investment debts. The company previously gave generous bonuses for many years. The staff had a bonus every month, also on the company anniversary and especially TET Holiday (Lunar New Year). After two years without them, people are understandably disappointed. But with Covid, you know, maintaining a full salary and providing a 13 or 14-month salary for over 300 people is a bit too much. But it's true that not maintaining bonus and salary increases was my fault. It's the CEO's fault for not doing well.

But ... the period prior flashed back: We had an idea: "Sara, our company wants to set up an office in New York; ask if anyone wants to work there. If anyone wants to invest together."

"Yes, let me ask."

At the end of the day, I asked again, "Sara, is there anyone who wants to work in the US?"

"No, David. No one wants to go to America. Maybe working at the office is too pleasant, being provided with so many services. No one wants to go, especially since the company brings a lot of traveling to Europe and America. No one wants to work overseas for such a long time."

The next day: "David, Lynda just came into my room to talk. She wants to go to America to work," Sara said.

"That's it! But she works in the Documents Department. How can she go?"

"Maybe we would have to train her."

"Hey Sara, remember to be clear. Recently, some people we invested in, to go to the fairs in Germany and the US ... We paid so much money for that. Then, after returning home, they just quit their jobs. We didn't even know what to do with them."

"Yes, let me arrange more detailed agreements."

Two days later, Sara came into my room and said. "I talked to Lynda, and she wants to go to the US to work, and if it is suitable, maybe she wants to live there in the future."

"That's great, but what about the deal?"

"Yes, I also said there was an agreement. She commits to work for the company for a time; otherwise she would have to pay compensation."

"So first let her learn operations and then sales. We have to train her carefully."

"Yes, let me talk to her and plan carefully."

Lynda called me from the US, saying, "New York is great, Manhattan is great too. Could you give me two days off so I can visit my relatives in California?"

"Okay, you can."

"Hi, I just got back from the US," Lynda called me. "How is everything?" I asked.

"Yes, I like it very much. I would also like to live there."

"Hey Sara, our company is quite good; we have the conditions to send employees everywhere in Europe, America and many other places," I happily called Sara and said.

"Yes, that's right, anyone who loves work and has the ability to work in our office will have opportunities for such great development," Sara replied.

Three years later: Lynda had just returned from America. "How are you? Did you visit your relatives in America?" I asked.

"Yes, but my relatives are all so uncordial, and I see everyone is either unemployed or working too hard. They can't save much. There are too many taxes and bills to pay in America, and people can barely save anything."

"Would you still like to live there?"

"Yes, I still like it."

A few days later, Sara came into my room to tell me, "David, I heard from Lynda that she's going to get married."

"Really? Good news! Where's her fiancé?"

"Yes, her boyfriend is an American from New York, an architect."

"So good," I replied.

A few months later, Lynda was back in America, and I got a call. "Boss," she said, "Covid here is too serious. The rate of people dying or getting stuck in hospitals is high, and there aren't enough ambulances. It's terrible."

"So, stay at home, don't go out. Buy everything online," I said.

"Lynda just called me," Sara said. "She was depressed. I have to talk to her all the time, so she won't be afraid."

"Well, everyone is like that; living alone is so scary. The students are coming back to the office next week, so it'll be more cheerful, though busier."

"Yes, it'll be more fun, but tiring."

They spent six months together in the New York office, cooking, shopping and many other things ... The mood was better but more tiring.

"Sir, I registered to return to Vietnam," Lynda called me and said.

"So, what about the students?"

"Yes, I'll go back first. They are adults, so they can take care of themselves. My visa is almost expired, so I have to go back to Vietnam," Lynda said.

Nine months after the start of Covid, the new Delta variant swept through the city I was living in. For the first time, we went into real lockdown. Many families and young people had to stay at home. That's when the real pressure started. So many quick decisions were made, and so many changes occurred.

For four years, I had hoped to be invited to Lynda's wedding. If not, at least to see a photo of the bride and groom. To see Lynda's joy and happiness, her American Dream coming true. But talking to Sara made me feel that this would not come true.

Sara pushed open the door to my office. She said, "I talked to Lynda today. She was so nervous and afraid it would all be too late if she didn't do it in time. She's coming home!"

"Really? So, she doesn't want to stay in America anymore? What about her fiancé? Did she give up on the American Dream?"

"I told her, but she just said that she only wants to go back to her hometown and take care of her family; now she doesn't care anymore ..."

Covid during lockdown days, September 3, 2021.

DOING BUSINESS DURING COVID

As usual, at the end of the year, I sit down and write a "To Do List" for the next year. This was the end of 2019, and the trips of 2020 were all going in completely unplanned directions.

It was early February 2020. The Covid situation had spread out of China. At the time, the information coming from Wuhan was intense. We had a fair in Dubai, the "Dubai Fair." The organizers were proceeding with their plans. There were many delegations from other countries registered to take part. However, near the date of the fair, many of them withdrew. We had to decide whether or not to go. The morning of our flight, we sat down again and decided we wouldn't risk going to the fair. We immediately contacted our partners and organizers to inform them we would not take part this time because the pandemic was complicated and risky. Looking back, we think it was the correct decision.

The International Peppercorn Conference was held in India in March. This time it was certain that we would not go, so we sent a letter to the organizers informing them we wouldn't be taking part. As expected, the organizers canceled the event at the end of the month. From March until now, the conventions have stopped because of the pandemic. How can we do business during Covid? I have witnessed three major crises, 1997, 2007–2008, and now the third crisis continues to this day. But with this crisis, our business was affected not so much. We were in the business of producing and exporting food and drinks. "Everyone has to eat," I thought. However, this crisis has really been terrible so far. As of now, we don't know if it will ever end. We can only try to cope with it by working hard and adapting every day.

When Wuhan locked down, I foresaw a difficult scenario. Even though Europe and the US were unaware of the danger at that time, I knew I had to work much harder. That way, if something happened, I would still have dry food to gradually consume. We strove every day, but things kept getting worse and worse. Initially, Italy and Spain locked down, then gradually, all countries. Our customers are mainly European, so everything seemed so difficult. But we all thought: "We don't have that many choices, do we? Just have to adapt."

So, we had to adapt to be able to sell our cargoes. We reviewed the entire list of customers we sold the bulk of our products to, then reached out to them. Fortunately, our policy for many years has been to have diversified customers. We are selling many products to small and medium-sized-customers. We are different; we build our profile of customers by mainly choosing mid-range ones with strong financial potential. When selling, I always choose customers who are not too big, as well as kind and responsible. Knowing how to say "no" is a very useful skill in business. The great advantage of the pandemic occurring now is that many people are choosing to shop on online channels and supermarkets. The amount of this type of buyer doubled or tripled compared to previous years. We focused on them and persisted in selling day and night. From January to April 2020, we increased sales orders by 30 percent in volume.

I consider myself lucky because, during Covid, everyone lost orders, lost jobs, reduced wages, got fired … But our factory is running full capacity. While our customers in many markets were in lockdown and could not come to the office, many factories, such as in India, Jordan and elsewhere, were essentially closed. At that time, we were exporters and sellers of food, so we could still produce and export cargoes. Since many people in other countries couldn't attend the office, unemployment grew and wages shrunk. Fortunately, we could still work full time and receive a full salary. There was even more work; it was great luck.

However, the waves of challenge never stopped. In May, everything changed. After the global closures had eased, all the customers who bought many batches at first did not need to buy from us anymore. The consumption decreased a great deal. Customers didn't order anymore. What now? What kind of approach do we take to selling and surviving?

However, everything changed within a few weeks, and because of the crisis, the supply was not full, so the price of goods began to rise again. Customers realized that if they did not buy soon, they would have to buy at higher prices later, when warehouses were almost empty. Companies immediately adapted by buying back goods to avoid price increases, instantly making the domestic price war fierce. It would be a long battle, and we knew we'd have to work hard every day …

The price war is still difficult, and we don't know when this pandemic will end, but we will die the moment we are negative and stop trying; as long as we strive and put in the effort, there is still hope.

FIERCE MARKET

Sometimes life changes in the most unexpected ways.

Usually, I go on business trips to meet customers for six months out of the year, diligently moving around airports and working ardently in places around the world. Now the pandemic has made it impossible to go anywhere. Phuc Sinh Consumer Corporation has been established for four years and managed by hired CEOs. During this time, we lost around US$2 million. The business results were bad, and everything was ruined. Their salaries were high, yet the returns they promised were fake. Who was to blame? I could only blame myself. So, from September 2019, I ran the company directly. When I had the time, I would carefully check details in order to solve any backlog for distributors, agents, and employees. I also dealt with scammers.

I focused on the business sales and distribution systems and launched many new products, such as Freeze-dried Green Peppercorn, Red Peppercorn, Cascara Blue Son La Tea, and Kfilter Blue Son La. Aside from the new products that were first sold in Vietnam, we focused on packaging design. Everyone has said that K Coffee has a much different packaging design than previous coffee products. My friends, who are newspaper editors, business owners, buyers and especially people in the industry, all say that K Coffee's packaging has changed how people see coffee packaging in Vietnam. It's not just black and red anymore, but colorful, beautiful, and artistic.

We strived on all fronts to survive, investing more in the online segment. We made improvements to allow customers to more easily place orders: simplifying the interface's aesthetic and finding the best ways to interact with customers. Our website www.kphucsinh.vn thus received more attention from customers. Orders increased.

We also tried to learn everything about product presentation, as a good product will not be bought without being introduced well. At the same time, the export segment was also focusing on the modern sales segment in the supermarket system. This all led to the display and distribution segment performing much better. Just like that, we strove day by day.

I saw myself as a collector of classic and beautiful art. So, on the occasion of the Mid-Autumn Festival, I thought of making beautiful coffee products ... like a painting. Happy Box was born, inspired by Van Gogh's famous *Starry Night*! It was a set of four products: Instant coffee for people who like to drink coffee with milk conveniently in the morning; Kfilter coffee for those who like to drink pure coffee that is ready in two minutes; filter coffee; and machine coffee of the two varieties "K Happy" and "K Life." We named it the "Happy Box" because we wanted everyone to feel happy. Looking at the beautiful, glittering, artistic coffee package indeed made me feel very happy. K Coffee's coffee is great, and the beautiful packaging makes it special. We hoped customers would love the beauty of the packaging and support our pure and delicious coffee. At first, I thought of it for the Mid-Autumn Festival specifically. But, when the "Happy Box" was born, it was not confined only to the Mid-Autumn Festival, but its beauty was suitable for any occasion; to gift to friends during Tet, for example. It is truly beautiful and artistic, and the price is very affordable.

We continued with such efforts, changing day by day to survive. The pandemic is still raging in Vietnam and many countries worldwide, yet I think we have no choice but to make efforts to overcome these difficulties. The pandemic has been a time for us to focus more on the domestic market, producing many beautiful and artistic products and having more time to care for friends, colleagues and families. Not only was I able to keep nearly 300 managers, officers and workers, but also to pay full salaries on time and continue recruitment efforts.

With the pandemic making us stay home, we found something meaningful to work on. If we didn't have so much time at home, perhaps we wouldn't have come up with such a beautiful and thoughtful idea as the "Happy Box" gift. Our online system is tended to and upgraded daily regarding customer service. These are all changes that, if considered from a year-end perspective, have been the most unexpected.

It's only August, and everything still lies ahead; striving every day …

END-OF-YEAR REFLECTION 1

At the end of each year, I sit down and reflect on what I have been both able and unable to achieve. I hope that what I haven't been able to do in the current year I could continue in the coming year. Here are a few short pieces to share my thoughts on the final days of this year.

Manhattan: Looking for Vietnamese Food

I would visit Manhattan in New York once or twice a year to visit customers. While there, I would Google Vietnamese restaurants and, strangely enough, couldn't find any in the city center! There are Thai and many Chinese and Korean restaurants. When I searched more carefully, I found Vietnamese restaurants outside the city. I called my friend to ask if he could suggest anything. He did, but when I went there, it had been sold and was now a Thai restaurant. There are a lot of Vietnamese in the US, but why are there so few in New York? And so few Vietnamese restaurants in the center of New York? I think it's probably because the business competition is so fierce there.

Regarding Korean food, Koreans have all of 32nd Street in Manhattan to sell their cuisine. If you want to eat a Korean barbecue, just go to 32nd Street. If you want to eat kimchi, just go to 32nd Street. There is even karaoke with barbecue. Koreans are hardworking and full of determination!

Startups and Other Degrees

Since we are talking about startups, I would like to tell a startup story about Korean companies and restaurant owners in Vietnam. I live in Phu My Hung, Hochiminh City where there are hundreds of Korean restaurants. Perhaps there are more of them than Vietnamese restaurants. On average, Koreans have little money when they immigrate to Vietnam. Many Korean families with children only have enough money to rent a house for five to seven months when they first come to Vietnam. The first thing is to rent a house, buy things for their shop, recruit Vietnamese staff and open a Korean restaurant. Their shops are very simple, yet clean. Waking up at 4 a.m., the owner goes to the market. They cook and serve customers from 10 a.m. to 11 p.m. The attitude toward service is very good: bowing and serving guests attentively. They train their staff very well, and the price is also quite affordable. When comparing natural conditions, Vietnam is a paradise compared to Korea. Nevertheless, Korea has great companies such as Samsung and Hyundai. For cars, sometimes Hyundai has the highest sales in the US.

Many Korean shop owners come to Vietnam with a modest amount of money to open a restaurant. They hire Vietnamese people for labor and teach them about service (I am just writing a true story and I don't think Vietnamese people will feel ashamed when they read it).

In Vietnam, we have been integrated for a long time. The proof is that we do not say, "we've just opened our door." We try to teach our children, so they may eventually go to university. That may be considered enough. Or to study further for a master's or doctorate degree. Winning any particular award would be honorable. But many forget what they've learned after all that education ... What kinds of products could they produce for themselves and for society? Beyond education is whether you can create something, like a startup, how many jobs you can provide, and how you can benefit society.

Learning is important, but it's only the beginning. That mindset is not taught in schools, and there's little talk about it. When the economy is open, we have to make a living. The startup model becomes something very abstract and far-fetched. Many people are used to having a university degree or higher. There's an idea that having a prestigious university degree is enough to just work in peace. Yet when the work runs out or circumstances force us to earn a living differently, this particular type of learner becomes confused and disoriented. The concept of integration is still not exactly stable, which is very challenging for many.

In fact, as I said, going to university or having a prestigious degree are just some of the first conditions for getting a good job. The main thing is making significant efforts to create good, innovative and competitive products for ourselves and society. This often takes a lifetime of striving. Thinking about quitting too soon makes it difficult to achieve success.

So, sometimes success depends on something inside a person. It's not always about having a lot of money, shouting slogans or having many degrees! At their beginnings, Samsung and Hyundai were not so rich.

On Collecting Art

As I've previously shared, I have been collecting paintings since 2012. And how, at the end of the year, I made a Tet calendar. I printed my collection and sent the calendars to clients. After receiving the calendar, there were many foreign business owners who, when talking about their trade, would end up talking about paintings. They'd ask me when I started collecting art. I would show them more Vietnamese paintings. Many people have loved Vietnamese paintings since I started sharing such works with them. Some would ask to purchase one for themselves, and I would ask the gallery to send better paintings. I sold a few paintings to customers this way. After four years of collecting art, I noticed many foreign business owners, from small to large, taking an interest and collecting and investing in paintings. That differs greatly from buying and collecting investment paintings in Vietnam.

Vietnam has many talented painters, but very few people who collect them are businesses, bankers and investment funds! We rely heavily on foreign customers, who inevitably drive the price up. How could we ask for fairness? In foreign countries, nearly all successful people leave an inheritance. In addition to money, real estate, etc., a very important and valuable category is the arts. This is almost nonexistent in Vietnam; you can count the instances on your fingers. The concept of integration is also very vague and far-fetched in collecting and investing in paintings.

My Hometown, Hai Phong

Hai Phong is an old port city. If you stay in the city center and go up to the foot of Lac Long bridge, Tam Bac Street or the streets of Tran Quang Khai, Hoang Dieu, etc., you will find it very similar to European streets. A closer comparison is the old quarter of Hanoi or Hoi An. The best part is that these streets are quiet, peaceful, and beautiful. There are many delicious breakfast, lunch, and dinner restaurants. Hai Phong experienced a long and prosperous development compared to the whole country, so the dishes maintain high quality standards.

But what I want to share is that I was not born in that center; I was born on the border between the city and the countryside. The area where I lived, where the rows of old French houses were built, has small sidewalks and roads. My memories of the subsidized years were not of richness, but peace. The streets actually had sidewalks for people. Now, there are no more sidewalks; the houses and shops are on the street in the neighborhoods of An Da, Quan Ba Mau and Ngo Gia Tu, Dong Khe, and many others. Traveling by foot has become extremely dangerous. Whenever I return to my hometown and walk around my old neighborhood, I feel unsafe. Unfortunately, I don't see anyone there addressing this issue.

Sidewalks make people feel safe walking or that their children can play safely. Furthermore, when shopping, it is advisable to go to the market. But presently, people just display everything out on the sidewalk, and even on the road, to sell food. Anyone who wants to buy something could even stop in the middle of the road, which is very dangerous. Emphasis on peace and safety no longer exists!

I don't think it is difficult to solve this, as long as we want to do it and are disciplined. We work and live not only to make money. I think pedestrian safety, shopping safety, and traffic safety are also things we hope for.

I've often wondered why I didn't express love for Hai Phong and didn't know the answer. Last weekend, I went back to my hometown to take part in my mom's death anniversary.

I was taken out by friends to eat porridge and rice cake. It felt great. Naturally, I wanted to write about Hai Phong, and hopefully Hai Phong will experience more progress in the coming years. Everyone can hope, right? Through this article, I think I have expressed a lot of love for Hai Phong! It's just waiting for the opportunity to rise.

A few lines at the end of the year, things, hopes and thoughts that remain. Despite everything, we always keep hope, don't we?

December 2016

DEBT COLLECTING

When I finish an initial story, I always want to write the next one, but writing is never easy. Writing requires emotion. Sitting down to write can be especially challenging if you are not a professional writer or journalist.

Since we wanted to sell coffee to the US market, we attended a coffee fair there. At such fairs, we always work hard, as there are often many customers.

While I bent down to prepare a sample, a man's voice rang out, "Hello! Coffee from Vietnam, right?"

"Hi guys, how are you? Yes, we are from Vietnam, and the coffee is as well."

The two men visiting Phuc Sinh's booth were customers from Colombia. Their country supplies Colombian Arabica Washed coffee, which is very famous around the world. Juan knew English and Alfonso spoke only Spanish.

We talked cordially, and they promised to visit us in Vietnam.

Two months after the trip, the phone rang.

"Hello, Minh, right? It's Juan. How are you? We are coming to visit you."

"Hello, Juan, I'm fine. When will you arrive?"

"In two weeks. Are you in Saigon?"

"Yes."

So we made an appointment to meet in Vietnam.

Two weeks later, our company car picked them up, took them to their hotel, and later to our company.

"Oh, Vietnam, our first time here."

"So, is it different from what you imagined about Vietnam?"

"So different! Lots of motorbikes, very bustling."

We talked about buying and selling and arranged to have dinner.

The next day, we drove them to our coffee factory.

"I want to buy Robusta coffee." They started negotiating.

"You want to buy coffee? I think Colombia has a lot of coffee already."

"Oh no, we export products to Europe and the US, but now South America also drinks instant coffee. We buy slightly lower quality Robusta for cheap and easy competition."

"Oh, the world is so good. South America comes to Vietnam to buy Robusta coffee, my god!"

We negotiated, and they bought 35 containers of class two and class three coffee. We also negotiated payment methods. They made a down payment and would pay the outstanding balance after delivery. Since the terms of the contract were in accordance with international practices, we decided to sell them coffee. Shipment and delivery began and payment was made as contracted.

After three months, I received an email. "Mr. Minh, we want to buy 92 containers with a partial shipment. Payment method being the same." After negotiating the price, we received the deposit and started the coffee delivery.

With this second purchase, the first 40 containers were paid for quite slowly, splitting each part. I eventually, finally, got 80 percent payment for the 40 containers. We still had the original shipping documents and deposit for the rest of the containers.

I called them. "Juan, please pay the balance for the 40 containers, then we will deliver?"

"Hello, Minh, don't worry, just make the delivery. You still keep the original shipping documents and 80 percent of the money. Please deliver 52 containers; we need the goods. We'll take care of the 20 percent payment for the first shipment on the sea. The ship is about to dock; we have to pay to pick up the goods."

I had a feeling that they were good people, so I told the guys at the office, "Give them 52 containers!" So our office delivered 52 containers.

A week later, due to a busy workload, we forgot to ask for the money. Fifty-two containers were loaded onto the mother ship from Singapore. I remembered the shipment and started asking for money.

"Hey Juan, how are you?"

"Hello, Minh, I'm fine."

"I still haven't received your money," I mentioned.

"Minh, let me check!"

"In that case, I'll call you back in 30 minutes!" I said, and we hung up.

Thirty minutes later, I called Juan, but no one answered or called back. Unable to contact him by phone, I emailed him, asking for payment.

The next day, I woke up, opened the email, and no reply. What's going on? It was late in Colombia, but I still called. The phone just rang with no answer. I felt quite worried and didn't know what to do.

The next day I called again, and Juan picked up the phone.

"Sorry, Minh, I'm too busy. I already checked; we will transfer the money by the end of the week!"

"Is that so? It's only Tuesday. Besides, you said you already transferred last week, right?"

"We have a little problem; I hope you can understand. We will definitely transfer the money to you this week; goodbye!" Juan hung up.

I wanted to talk more, but the phone was already hung up, so I had to wait. The sum of money was nowhere near insignificant, and we were worried. The next day, I kept calling and Juan didn't pick up. The following day, I called, and Juan picked up but said he was in a meeting and would call back. I kept waiting, but no calls came back. I didn't know what to do! His friend Alfonso couldn't speak English. I felt extremely worried. Thursday, when I called, Juan picked up the phone immediately and said the money was paid and we would receive it tomorrow. I was extremely happy.

The first thing I thought of when I woke up was the money. I looked forward to 11 a.m. to check the bank. While I was dealing with work, the staff from the Finance Department called me to say that I had received money from the customer from Colombia. They paid the 20 percent of the old debt and part of the 52-container lot. I was relieved, as the money had finally come. Moreover, I was partly more confident since the 52-container lot had been partially paid.

Yet, there was still a portion of the shipment value that had not been paid in full. I waited a week, then started asking for money again. Juan picked up the phone and said the situation was not good, but they would try to pay. I asked when, and Juan told me to take it slowly for them to make arrangements.

On Thursday, I called. It was bad news:

"Minh, my buyer is having difficulty in paying us. However, we will try to pay you," Juan said.

I was very worried. The 52 containers were nearing the South American port, and I'd only received 30 percent payment.

The next day I called Juan, but no one answered. I called the company, and the staff said Juan was on a business trip. I sat down and thought about what to do. How could I claim this money? Suddenly I remembered Juan had an office in Japan, and I had written down the number. I called Juan there. On the other end, a Japanese employee told me to wait a minute. Then Juan was on the other line. After talking for a while, I asked about the payment. Juan asked me to let him check and call me back. I said it'd been too long and asked why he didn't pay me. Juan repeated that he would check again. An hour later, I called back, no answer. I called again, once every hour, and still couldn't get through.

The next day, feeling really worried, I called Juan and, just like the previous times, couldn't get through. For an entire week, things continued like that; we demanded money and tried to find another method. I assumed they were probably decent people. This situation was likely due to the financial difficulties of their customers. But it would be very difficult for us if we couldn't claim the money. It was a lot of money! Just like that, I called Juan. Lucky for me, I finally reached him.

"Juan, how are you? I kept calling but couldn't reach you."

"Minh, I'm fine. I have bad news, though; my buyer has gone bankrupt. I was just helping Alfonso. I'm so tired!"

"Why didn't you say this when you started the deal? And only you can speak English. Alfonso can't speak English. How could we trade? I am very worried."

"I don't know, Minh. My family is ruined because you kept calling all the time, and I'm really just helping Alfonso. Please arrange it yourself! Okay?"

"Juan. Listen to me, listen to me …" The line was dead!

Alfonso only knew how to say "Hello" and "How are you?" That was it. He couldn't speak more than that, and I didn't speak Spanish! What then? Withhold the stock? The goods had already arrived! If I flew over to Colombia, what would be the use? I still didn't know any Spanish. What could I do …?

I had many nice customers in Spain, but asking them to collect money for me was a very different thing.

Or should I ask them to write a letter in Spanish demanding money? Once, twice, and for a third time, I shied away, as it would surely affect our business relationship with these companies.

I couldn't sleep and kept thinking. Then an idea flashed: Google!

I woke up at 2 a.m., which was within South American business hours. I wrote an email in English, translated it into Spanish on Google, and sent it to Alfonso. Then I waited. I wrote in a simple, easy-to-understand manner. I explained my difficulty with the bank if we didn't get paid. Miraculously, I received a letter in Spanish from Alfonso. He told me not to withhold the goods; he was paying me and I would receive the money by next Tuesday at the latest.

Tuesday morning, I got up early. I still had to run a company that exports hundreds of containers each month and did everything as usual, and waited.

After many months of waiting, I got a call from the bank. The Deputy Director of International Payments was the one who called.

"Minh, the money you told me to keep an eye out for has arrived. Money from Colombia."

"Is that so? I'm so happy; let me check it out." I checked with the Finance Department, and the amount corresponded to 15 percent of the shipment value.

I was overjoyed! Everything felt so light, like I had just gotten out of a black hole, and I had more faith.

I continued waking up every night to write emails and use Google to translate. Then to receive emails, use Google to translate and connect with Alfonso.

"Dear Alfonso, why haven't you paid? The bank keeps asking, what should I do?"

"Minh, we will pay tomorrow."

The following day would come and I would contact the bank. "Has the company received any money from Colombia?"

"No, Minh ..."

The situation went on and on, never knowing when it would end.

However, after persisting for four months, we got 85 percent.

The remaining 15 percent stayed stagnant, which made me so tired. They promised to pay by Thursday. When I woke up on Friday, the first thing I did was check my mail again. There was a text message with an apology for not paying yet! I was so tired; I lay in bed and got sick! I developed a high fever, yet I felt fine right before receiving the news. Sometimes, when faith is exhausted, the resilience in a person is also weakened.

A week later, also on a Friday, it was finally paid after all that work with Google translate trying to collect money. Plus, I received interest on deferred payments.

This is a dream! I thought to myself! All the feelings of being abandoned for four months came rushing back: staying up all night writing emails, persevering, and keeping a strong faith. Finally, the money was paid. I felt sorry for myself because when things were difficult, only I knew. I fought on. Customers, partners and employees expected my perfection and professionalism at all times, but silently I struggled with the pressure of all this.

Business has always been a battle of wits, a persistent fight: managing and processing to gain money to pay countless bills, always having to pay attention to the due batches. Some customers automatically pay, but many customers must always be pushed if you want them to pay on time. And when there's a problem, you can't tell anyone.

I told my friend, "I feel sorry for myself!"

"My gosh, Minh! You have a house, a car, a company and helpers! There are many people who work their asses off, and you sit here and pity yourself!"

Yes, maybe people didn't understand my persistence in business and how I have to fight alone with my customers and the market. In this situation, the big problem for both of us – as the seller and the buyer – is not only the geographical distance and lack of information on both sides, but that neither of us could understand what the other was saying. We still had to overcome it. A special skill in business is the ability to assess the trustworthiness of customers.

Looking back on the over four-month period of debt collection, I know I may not have had to work so hard because there were still other options. If I had chosen those options, I would have directly destroyed the business of my clients, causing them to lose a lot. I could have taken back the goods to sell because I still had the original contract documents, and the customer could not have asked me for compensation as they had made me wait too long. However, I chose cooperation and trust in people. In the end, I got good results.

Sometimes difficulty strengthens us and makes us more energetic. Sometimes difficulty makes us more creative. When I met Alfonso again in Houston, we used Google translate to invite each other to dinner and chat. After all this, I think God had tested my patience and creativity in business – which was an experience as colorful as life itself!

NARROWLY ESCAPING FRAUD

Köln, Germany, on an October day.

In the morning, we went to the Anuga fair. We were ready for a busy day; we got up early, got on the train and hit the road. This was the first day of the fair, and everything – goods and catalogs – had to be well-prepared. We needed to be in high spirits to welcome potential new customers. After a few people had visited our booth, we picked up a visitor from Europe. He looked very smart with a black briefcase, like an Eastern European.

"Hello, how are you?" I asked.

"I'm fine. How are you?" he replied.

"I'm fine too. How can we help you?" I asked.

"May I introduce myself? My name is Mike Tyson. Our company name is Varna, and we are from Bulgaria. I am interested in Vietnamese black peppercorn. Every year, we import a large quantity and look for companies who can steadily supply this for us."

"Well, that's our forte! We have traveled a long way to bring peppercorn to this exhibition."

We were excited to introduce Vietnamese black peppercorn to this Bulgarian customer. After reviewing everything – the types and specifications of peppercorn, the factory, the price – we parted and promised to reach out and do business together after the fair.

Like all guests, we saved this man's business card, noted the specific needs mentioned, and continued with our work. Anuga is the largest food and beverage fair on the planet. The fair has eight large zones. It's so big that you wouldn't even be able to visit the whole place in five days. In other words, you can always lose your way once you've left your booth. We received hundreds of guests each day; five people worked continuously from 9 a.m. to 6 p.m. without even having lunch. Guests from all around the world were interested in Vietnamese spices and coffee. Here, we get a chance to meet with old clients every two years; if they haven't come to visit Vietnam or we haven't visited them in their country.

There were many guests. We talked about health, business, and, if we were really close, family and children. There were some interactions when the guest left us with an invitation.

"Well, we have a dinner scheduled. I made a reservation for dinner at a place near the river in Köln. Are there five people with you?"

"Yes, we have five people."

"See you in the evening!"

The Anuga fair is where to meet old customers and get better acquainted. It is also the place to build new customer relationships. So, every two years, Anuga is a place where people meet, discuss business, and then say goodbye with the hope of continued contact.

After five days, the fair ended, and we flew back to Vietnam. When we returned to Saigon, we immediately started to contact people we had met at the fair. We arranged meetings and assigned staff to look after their accounts.

I had a long list of emails and offers to send: a week's worth of continuous work with customers, inquiries and answers. At the end of the week, a customer with whom I had never dealt, but had met at the fair, sent me an email and fax asking for a large quantity of peppercorn. They wanted to buy 50 containers of peppercorn. Wow! Why so large? The order also detailed the types of goods and specifications. Most notably, they required immediate delivery.

I called him and said, "Hello, Mike Tyson. I received your email and fax asking about peppercorn."

"Hello, you are Mr. Quang, right? Yes, I need to buy peppercorn."

"The order is rather large. Do you really want to buy 50 containers worth of peppercorn? When should it be delivered?"

"Yes, we need a large quantity."

"Have you ever bought Vietnam's peppercorn before?"

"No, this is the first time."

"Really?" I was surprised. "Do you really want to buy 50 containers worth of peppercorn?" Such an order was too large for the peppercorn industry, especially for immediate delivery. How could it be done? It was November then. The main peppercorn crop yields from February to July every year. We checked and looked for goods from suppliers and partners. In the end, we found 30 containers.

"Hi Mike, it's very difficult at the moment to find a large quantity of peppercorn. Thirty containers is the best we can do."

"Oh, we need 50 containers. Can you try to find the rest?" he tried to convince me.

"Mr. Quang, we need this large quantity for a United Nations order; please try to find it!"

I found Mr. Tyson to be earnest, so I tried to find more. Considering that we are an export business, we must sell to make money to run the business! After five consecutive days of searching ...

"Hi Mike, how are you? I have good news, I found 37 containers. This is the most I can do; it cannot be more. The price is US$6,400 per ton CNF[3] Varna, Bulgaria."

"Is that so, Mr. Quang? You can't find more? Why is the price so expensive?"

"This price is good, right now the freight price is not cheap!"

"Come on, take US$6,200 per ton."

"No, peppercorn is very expensive now. The best price I can do is US$6,300 per ton."

After negotiating for a while, the customer accepted that price. However, while negotiating payment conditions, many red flags arose. We usually require a 20 percent down payment in advance and the rest when we fax the export documents.

---

3 CNF price includes products and freight, stands for Cost and Freight.

But they refused, insisting on 100 percent C.A.D.[4] via their bank. This was too risky. With a shipment of US$3,263 million (nearly 53 billion VND), it was not easy to give the nod to this when I had only met them once at the fair. In such a case, and with my *current* experience, I would fly to them and talk. However, that was 2007 and I was young and inexperienced. The company was only five years old.

"Hi Mike, this order is too large! We need payment before delivery."

"Hi, Mr. Quang. We are in Europe, and all payments are made by bank collection here."

"No, Mike. We can't do it if we don't get at least 10 percent in advance. Sorry, but I have to decline if I don't receive at least 10 percent, and the rest paid via fax voucher. It's hard to get groceries these days, and it's difficult to have that much cash, Mike. I have to take out a loan from a bank, and the bank considers a contract with no prepayment clause as not loanable."

"Mr. Quang, let me negotiate with the management of Varna Company."

Two days later:

"Mr. Quang, we agree to pay 10 percent in advance. Send me your bank details, and we will transfer."

"Good. I'll get the office to send you the bank info."

I asked the Varna staff to sign the contract. When it was confirmed, I instructed my staff to send Varna the bank details so they could transfer the money.

We were extremely pleased to receive their advance, and now it was time to prepare this huge shipment. The money they had advanced was 10 percent. The rest they insisted on paying through their bank. Their bank collection was not a bad idea: The bank would deliver the documents if they had money to pay. If not, the bank kept the documents; that was the C.A.D. method. We contacted the bank repeatedly to ask

---

4 C.A.D. (Cash Against Document): Payment method for documents.

about the security of the payment, and the bank said that if the requesting bank was legitimate, it would be quite safe. We were satisfied with the initial step and started to buy 37 containers of peppercorn. When working with agricultural suppliers, we must pay them the full price to get the goods.

However, once we agreed to the payment method, we received a call. After the initial greetings, the conversation went as follows:

"Mr. Quang, we want to buy the peppercorn for Varna, Bulgaria, but pay you via Turkey."

"How so?"

"My client has money in Turkey and wants to pay from there. It's okay, Mr. Quang. I buy other items as well. Just rest assured."

"Let me check it out."

We contacted the bank, and they said it was okay, payment being the same anywhere as long as the paying bank is legitimate.

So, we agreed. The goods were purchased under CIF[5] Terms to Varna, with the collection and payment handled by the bank in Turkey. With little experience, we didn't think much of this detail, which put us in great danger later on.

The bank we used for services was Vietcombank (VCB). They had warned us that this was a large transaction and asked the buyer to provide the bank's name. We did just that. The name of the Turkish bank was quite famous, high ranking and safe. We confirmed and drew up the sales contract. Selling 37 containers worth of black peppercorn at US$6,300 per ton was the largest contract with us at that time. Large regarding both sales and onetime delivery.

I received a call from Mr. Tyson:

"Hello, Mr. Quang. Have the goods been delivered yet?"

"Yes, they have, Mike."

---

5 CIF stands for terms of delivery, which means delivery at the port of discharge: Cost, Insurance, Freight. It is often written with a certain seaport name, for example: CIF Haiphong.

"Are the documents done yet?"

"We are processing them."

"When you have the waybill for sending documents, let me know."

"Okay. We will inform you when we have it."

A few days later, the phone rang. "Hi, Mr. Quang. Do you have the waybill number?"

"Not yet, Mike."

"Why is it taking so long?"

"When I have it, I will send it to you straight away."

The next day, it was the same. They were constantly hounding us for the waybill number. We sensed something suspicious. Why would they ask so many times for the waybill? Was there a problem? There was only one set of documents for 37 containers of goods. Handing over those documents too soon could lead to us losing everything. If the customer acquired the documents, they could take the goods. I had to be careful, I told myself.

Mike called again, and I could only say that the bank was checking the documents because the shipment was so large. "Let us check with the bank. When the number is available, we will notify you."

Aside from our initial hunch, I read somewhere about a scam involving a courier number. To be sure, we met with our staff and informed the relevant departments, "You are not allowed to share the bill of lading number with these customers." I was to be the only one to notify them.

We sent the collection documents via VCB, and they used DHL services to send the documents to the Turkish bank.

Three days later, DHL informed us that the Turkish collection bank said they had no customers named Varna, and the collection's value was too large. The bank did not want to process it.

"Mike, the bank said they don't have any customers named Varna."

"Is that so? They must be mistaken. Let us check again …" Mike continued, "Mr. Quang, tell DHL to come back. Someone is waiting at the bank. Please give me the waybill number as well!"

"Mike, the bank also didn't give me the waybill number yet," I answered tersely for him to let me check with my bank.

I immediately held a meeting with the entire company and repeated: "No one is to give the waybill number to this customer!" I felt anxious.

The shipment was too big for us. I thought it would have been nice if we could have divided this lot into five sets!

"Mr. Quang. Do you have the waybill number?"

"Not yet, Mike."

"Okay, here's another bank name."

"Okay, Mike. I'll inform our bank."

We asked VCB to check, and they confirmed this bank was good. So, we asked VCB to send the collection documents to this bank. Meanwhile, I kept receiving emails, faxes and phone calls asking for my DHL number. We just replied that we had to check with the bank and would let him know later. However, in the meantime, I had a hunch that this customer wasn't being honest.

Two days later, VCB received a call from the new Turkish bank. They received the set of documents, but they found Varna wasn't their customer. Since they felt there was a scam, they sent us back the documents. We received a phone call from the bank expressing great concern.

A day later, the documents arrived in Saigon. Holding the documents in my hand, I was full of fear and joy!

Business was like that. The shipping company announced that the ship had docked at the port of Varna, Bulgaria. The goods would be unloaded and stored at the port there.

"Hello, Mr. Quang? Mike here. Have the documents already arrived in Vietnam? I heard from the bank that they have returned the documents."

I was strangely calm.

"Mike, let me check, then I will answer. But why did both banks say that Varna was not their customer?"

On the other end of the line, he grew a bit confused. "Let me check again ..." then the phone beeped, and no one was there.

Once we retrieved the documents, we felt that this was surely a scam. It was a close call. The next step we had to take was to transport these 37 containers out of the port in Varna, Bulgaria. As I mentioned before, our company had only been established for five years. This involved a large amount of money, almost all of it borrowed. Also, in 2007 there was a global crisis, and the prices of many things in my industry, as well as many other industries, fell drastically. Real estate fell drastically, and there were very few buyers. This scam occurred around the same time as the global crisis. That really messed everything up. I reminded myself to be very calm.

The phone rang. "Hello?"

"It's Mike Tyson. Let me speak to Mr. Quang!"

"Here I am. What do you want me to help you with?"

"You have received the shipment documents, right?"

"Shipment documents? Today is a day off. When I return to work, I will check with the bank and reply."

The next day:

"Hello, have you received the documents yet?"

"Today is still a holiday in Vietnam. I will contact you later."

Thirty minutes later: "Hello, Mr. Quang. I checked, and currently Vietnam does not have a public holiday."

After many more phone calls, I knew they discovered we were holding the original set of documents. The amount after deducting the deposit was more than US$2.9 million, a large amount. The global crisis made people even more afraid. I witnessed a lot of businesses that had started full of joy in 2005 and 2006. But in 2007 everything started to become difficult. The crisis peaked in 2008, and it swept worldwide. Many people lost everything that had taken them years to build. Some people were admitted to hospital because they couldn't stand the pressure; They were full of despair! Seeing them lose everything scared me.

In the same year, a neighbor of mine had a real estate brokerage company. Every morning we used to talk to each other.

"How is your job these days?"

"I'm so tired. I've lost it all! All those years of working my fingers to the bone ..." He was tattered, broken and empty!

"I'm also involved in a difficult case, trying to solve it calmly! I only have two things to do: sleep and work. When I work, I calmly handle the work. I have a large shipment I need to get out of the port of Varna." I told him my story.

"God, can you even sleep?"

"Oh, I can still sleep, just waking up a little earlier."

Looking back now, I think he was right. What if I got scammed? What then? I would have nothing left. To have lost everything, all those years of building. Even if we had to sell all our real estate during such a crisis, how much would we even make!

I tried not to think that way, and to be more optimistic. Thinking too much was just tiring and solved nothing.

At the office, we found a way to deliver the goods. The carrier ZIM Line, which did transportation for us, said that the goods had been unloaded at the port of Varna. There had to be a company to do the return procedures, though everything was not nearly as simple as I thought. It is true that we continuously learn in life, and we learn from our mistakes. But making such a big mistake would drown us, end the company and finish me!

During difficult times, I believe I must not panic. I must remain alert because wrong decisions can cost a great deal. Shipping lines only carry. They are not as good at coordinating as logistics companies. Instead of using shipping lines, I decided to use logistics. We contacted a very large logistics company in Europe at the time, Damco. Damco is a logistics company founded by Maersk in Denmark to coordinate and distribute goods worldwide. We went and talked to them.

The chief representative was Mr. Samuel, from India. Listening to our presentation, he was very interested. This was very good business for them, as it was the main trade of logistics companies.

"Mr. Quang, the first thing is authorizing the entire shipment to us."

"Oh my god, Samuel. Does that mean handing over the shipment to you guys? Over US$2.9 million!"

"Of course, we must be authorized to process the shipment. Trust us; it's our job."

"What about service prices?"

"Oh, we'll get a fair price. After we finish this meeting, I will negotiate with the office and offer you a very reasonable price."

We left, hearts full of doubt. Was it okay to delegate such a large shipment to Damco? What if they … However, I thought Damco was a big company, therefore, likely reliable. Without authorization, the goods cannot be retrieved.

A day later, we received an offer from Damco. After a little negotiation, we completed all the formalities and hoped that five days later, a ship would leave Varna for Hamburg.

Two days later, I received a phone call from Samuel at 11 p.m.

"Mr. Quang, Damco was doing customs procedures when your old buyer came with a lawyer. They gave evidence of a 10 percent advance and wanted to keep the goods. We are handling it and will contact you soon."

After hearing the news, I felt as if my heart had jumped out of my chest, and I worried about the shipment being held. I thought about it almost all night, just waiting until morning to contact them.

The next day, I went to the office to thoroughly check my emails. I hadn't received anything from Damco.

Nine o'clock: "Hi, Samuel. How are you?"

"That's it? Oh my gosh, what a relief! When does the freight leave?"

"Three more days."

We anxiously waited for the next three days. When something goes wrong, you have little time to deal with other things because you are waiting for the issue's status the whole time.

Three days later, we contacted to see how the shipment was coming along.

"Hi, Samuel. How are the goods?"

"Hi, Mr. Quang. Sorry, I was going to inform you. The ship omitted Varna port, so it did not enter the Varna port to receive the goods. I'm sorry, but there's nothing I can do!"

"Oh my god, what's wrong?" I almost lost my mind. "When is the next freight?"

"Another week, Mr. Quang."

"What? One more week?" I was going to say that I couldn't stand it and the old buyer could keep the goods, but I promptly kept silent. If they kept the goods, I'd be held accountable for nearly US$2.9 million. With all the money borrowed from the bank, at this time the interest rate in Vietnam dong was 18 to 22 percent per year. The more I thought about it, the more scared and desperate I became!

A week passed. I tried to work and not think too much about it. I had to work hard. I'm a CEO. I had to stay calm because everyone looked at me: employees, partners, customers, and banks. I couldn't show them my weakness! I just couldn't! That's the CEO's responsibility! Life's like that sometimes; we have to internalize our troubles!

I endured a week with patience and tried to focus on trading other shipments, running the office and dealing with the banks. In short, trying to do everything to keep the business going.

However, as the end of the week approached, I had a hard time sleeping. At the end of the week, I woke up to an email with a brief message.

"Hello, Mr. Quang. The shipment has been loaded. Our office will send you all the details later." A stream of cool oxygen flowed through my chest. Business is like that; sometimes you have to face something dangerous. The important thing is whether you have enough intelligence, insight and courage to deal with the problem or not.

I held an office meeting to share the details of the incident. The next goal was determining where and how to sell and ship these 37 containers. What followed will be told in the next story.

March 2008

DIFFICULTY IN DOING BUSINESS
(NARROWLY ESCAPING FRAUD 2)

1. The first story

"Hi, Nam. Are you in the office? I want to come over to talk with you for a bit. I have something that I need your help with."

"Okay, come over." The phone exchange made me quite nervous.

"My company has just lost a full set of original documents in Turkey, and the customer has already picked up the goods without paying the money."

"Why don't you just fly over there?" I asked.

"I did fly over there but couldn't do a thing. The bank didn't help, and DHL only paid US$100 per document."

"So what should you do?"

"It's all gone, Nam. 5x40' peppercorn FCL[6] was too much for us!"

"So, what can I help you with?" I asked.

"Could you try to contact your customer there? Is there any way you can help me?" he replied.

He sat down briefly, calmly had a cup of tea, and told his story: "We sold to Turkish customers and shipped the goods. My bank sent the documents to the buyer's bank for collection. The customer cutely asked me for the DHL number, so my office gave it to them. Having the DHL number, they tracked the documents, stole them and took the goods. When I realized this and flew over, the bank there was oblivious. The consul and the police couldn't do anything. Can you see if there's any way you can help me?"

---

6 FCL (Full Container Load), is a term used in the shipping service for the size of the container weight.

2. The second story

"Hello, Fred. How are you?"

"Hello, Nam, I'm fine. How are you?"

"I'm fine, too. I have some business that I want to share with you to cooperate with and see if there's anything we can do together. Our client wants to buy 3x40' FCL of peppercorn with a 10 percent advance payment. The rest is to be paid through C.A.D. by the bank. We can divide the profit in half: after shipping, you pay me, and then you will claim the balance from the customer. What do you think?"

"So, how much does each side get?"

"US$100 per ton."

"That's good. Let's do it."

So, we shipped the peppercorn to the end customer in Turkey, and Fred's company in Singapore paid us. Later they will charge the Turkish customer.

After the shipment was loaded:

"Nam, have you loaded the shipment?" Tom Cruise, the Turkish customer asked.

Nam replied, "Let me check …" and after a few minutes, he said, "Yes, it's done."

"When will you send the documents to our bank?" Tom asked.

"Let me check with Fred in Singapore."

Nam sent the documents to Fred's company when the export procedure was finished. And then they sent the documents through HSBC Hong Kong to the buyer's bank for collection.

"Hello! Nam, do you have a DHL number?" Tom asked.

"Let me ask Fred."

Tom was very cunning. He did not ask me but rather asked our staff to request the DHL number. The staff immediately asked the Singapore fellow for the DHL number without thinking and then he gave it to Tom.

A week later, Fred called from Singapore:

"Nam, HSBC Bank informed us that the customer's bank did not receive the documents. When I looked at the website of the shipping lines, I found that the customer had already picked up the goods ..."

"So, what? They stole the documents! Call HSBC Hong Kong now to tell them." Nam told Fred.

Two days later, HSBC Hong Kong contacted the buyer's bank. They called the police, and the police finally found the culprits and arrested them.

"Oh, my god!" I exclaimed. "Lucky it wasn't lost. So much money!"

Two years later, after working with the bank, the buyer, the police, and Fred's company lawyer, we got the goods back. However, Fred's side had lost a lot of money to pay for all the expenses.

3. The third story

At the world's largest fair for agricultural products:

"Hi, sir. My name is Mike Tyson. We want to buy peppercorn in bulk."

"Hi, my name is Nam. What kind of peppercorn do you want to buy and how much is the yield?"

"I want to buy peppercorn 550 gram per liter clean. Fifty containers," Mike said.

"Really? It's quite large; let me check," Nam replied.

A week later, after returning from the fair, we were very busy. Mike called, "Hello, Nam."

"Hello Mike, yes."

"Do you remember my request?" Mike asked.

"I remember, Mike. We're looking into it."

Two days later:

"Hello, Nam. Have you been able to gather my order yet?"

"Hi Mike, I got it! Thirty-seven containers."

After a week, we finally agreed on a contract, 10 percent prepaid and the rest through bank collection. The goods shall be shipped to Varna, Bulgaria and collection documents shall be sent to Turkey.

"Nam, are the documents done yet?"

"Hello, Mike. Yes, done."

"Then send me your DHL number," Mike said.

I found something suspicious, and I felt I did not trust this guy when he kept calling me to take the DHL number. I had a staff meeting and instructed the staff not to send the DHL number to Mike. The bank Mike sent us for the collection was also the wrong one.

"Mike, the bank you sent was incorrect; please give us the correct bank."

"Wait a minute, Nam. Here is the bank. I already sent you a fax."

We sent the info to the bank, and after five days, our bank received a message back from the foreign bank saying that Varna was not their customer and the bill was too large. They said they thought this was a scam and immediately returned the documents to our bank.

"Oh, my god. So scary. I cannot imagine what my life would have been like if I had lost this set of documents …"

I dared not think further. At the same time, Mike kept calling me, and I picked up the phone.

On the other end: "Hello, Nam. It's Mike. I heard my bank returned the documents to you?"

"Hi Mike, today is a day off. When I go back to work tomorrow, I will check." I was, in fact, being quick-witted.

The phone rang again: "Hello, Nam. I just checked. Vietnam does not have a holiday today."

Just like that, we tried to process each other's information. I immediately met with all my staff and found a way to bring 37 containers back to Vietnam. But, when the ship left the port of Varna, I thought, why don't we find a way to sell all the peppercorns? Finally, I managed to sell 27 containers to customers in France, Israel and Germany and brought ten containers back to Vietnam.

Four weeks later, Tuan, an assistant, knocked on my door and said, "Mr. Nam, the goods have arrived in Ho Chi Minh City. When we sold it, it was U$6,200 per ton; now it has increased to US$6,500 per ton. What a blessing in disguise."

"I wouldn't want a blessing like that. It hurts my heart," I replied.

I opened the meeting room window; the sky was blue and cloudless. "Today is another exciting day!" I said and continued to look at the trading screen. Both the price of peppercorn and coffee had increased.

"Have a great day!" A message from a French customer who bought peppercorn containers wrote. "The peppercorn containers you sold me were good, Nam. Thank you!"

"Yes, thank you!" I said goodbye and resumed my business.

The story was written in two years and completed on 21 September 2021, during Covid-19 lockdown.

UNIQUE BUSINESSES

I still remember the difficult first years of doing business, always trying to find a way to survive. One time I went to Indonesia, a country that produces white peppercorn. They've been in white peppercorn production for 100 years, but Vietnam started planting fairly recently, from 2000 onwards. The question in my mind was: How could they have made white peppercorn all that time, and we couldn't? The question haunted me constantly, so I decided to invest my own money and buy a container of black peppercorn, then ask the producer to make white peppercorn for me. Based on how I saw the Indonesians make white peppercorn, we discussed how best to do this, but we were not to copy the method completely. If successful, we would split the profit in half. But, if we lost, Phuc Sinh would bear the risk at its own cost. After many failed attempts and wanting to give up, luck came to us. It took a few years of marketing to convince customers, but we finally succeeded.

Customers purchased and paid good prices. Ten years later, from a country that did not originally export white peppercorn, 25 percent of the peppercorn quantity exported to the world was white. We made money and built our first factory in 2005. After two to three years, everyone followed suit on how we produce Vietnamese white pepper, and our profits fell back to normal.

We were also the first company to sell jumbo pepper in Vietnam. We used to sell it in bulk, but then I thought: "Why shouldn't we take Jumbo peppercorn, put it in beautiful packaging, and sell at a high price?" Convincing our customers, we opened a new line of peppercorn for the Vietnamese people.

As the leading company opening direct exports to buyers worldwide, Phuc Sinh has inspired many private and state-owned enterprises to directly market and sell products everywhere.

We also created a wave of Vietnamese businesses confidently trading agricultural products worldwide.

In 2015, we saw an opportunity in the domestic coffee business. In our country at the time, all instant coffee was mixed with corn, soy, buttermilk and flavoring chemicals. Why couldn't we sell 100 percent pure coffee? So we started working. I must say it was a great idea! We advertised on TV during the Euro Championship. After only a few months, other brands also started to see this as a great idea and copied it. Our problem at that time was there was no distribution system. People who wanted to buy didn't know where to buy from. However, the foundational character of these imitators, both large and small, was not pure. It was difficult to imitate. Later, we gradually built up many distribution channels and opened online sales on www.kphucsinh.vn. We tried every possible way to provide products to consumers. Until now, K Coffee is the only roasted and ground coffee brand that can honestly state on the package: "100 percent pure."

Blue Son La, A Spontaneous Story!

Son La had grown delicious coffee for 35 years, but selling the product was very difficult. No one knew about the quality of excellent coffee products in this place. The Provincial Secretary often had to go to Dak Lak coffee festivals to invite big companies to invest in Son La. However, we did not get to see him at that time.

In 2017, I went to the Northwest to visit my friends and went to Son La. I knew coffee was grown in Son La, but that was all I knew. When I arrived, I was surprised to see that they planted so many coffee trees there. It was immense! One hundred percent Arabica. I built a Son La Arabica processing factory there. Thus, K Coffee Blue Son La Arabica was born. It is quite a unique product, with special beans from the far Northwest region, processed by modern machinery purchased from the most famous Arabica region in the world – Colombia! A funny fact: Many people living in the North, very close to Son La (such as Hanoi or Hai Phong), did not know that Son La had coffee, or that coffee was even grown in Son La before we launched this product! When it came to coffee, they only thought of the Central Highlands. However, not only does Son La grow coffee, but this coffee is the best in Vietnam. Son La has four seasons: spring, summer, autumn and winter. The harsh weather makes it difficult for the fruit to survive, but the quality is delicious and fragrant once it is crystallized.

Drunk on Peppercorn – A Unique Creation

We have had many glorious years with peppercorn, but the price has been low in recent years, and business has been full of challenges. I always thought about how to overcome it. Peppercorn sauce was born after going to the supermarket in Frankfurt, Germany. After that, freeze-dried peppercorn was also researched, processed and produced. It must be said that freeze-dried peppercorn has brought much joy and pride to Vietnam. There was no such thing in the world; we were the first country to produce and distribute this product.

Phuc Sinh was the first to create and distribute it. For a year now, we have been exporting to the US, Switzerland, and Dubai, among others. Now, after a year of exporting only freeze-dried green peppercorn products, we are back to supplying this peppercorn to the domestic market in Vietnam. Seeing beautiful products is great, and consumers are buying them joyfully.

After building a peppercorn factory, white peppercorn and other products (such as freeze-dried peppercorn, a delicious and beautiful quality spice product, like a work of nature) brought profit for me. Then, the glittery, beautiful Blue Son La brought the brand to the Northwest region of Son La. All of this has been a source of pride. I realized that I had done well enough, but if I hadn't, I would still always have found a way to exist and develop.

END-OF-YEAR REFLECTION 2

We are a raw coffee manufacturer, which is also known as green coffee, or "green bean coffee." We produce about 60,000-70,000 tons annually, equivalent to 3,000-3,500 containers. We are also one of Vietnam's largest black peppercorn exporters, and doing domestic business is both responsible and attractive. Being a B2B[7] business but continuing to sell consumer goods like B2C[8] was a reality gap I didn't realize at the time. It also proved to be a difficult journey for me over the upcoming time period.

The coffee industry was full of tension and fluctuation. Coffee prices in both London and New York fell to the lowest level in the last 15 years, pushing farmers, exporters and traders into a tough situation and struggling to survive; 2019 was even more difficult for traders and coffee exporters worldwide.

Normally, the price of raw materials from the producing countries would also decrease. But, in this case, it went up. The people of the producing countries decided not to sell at low prices.

Previously, coffee growers in Vietnam stored their coffee at warehouses or sold it to traders. Now, they started to keep coffee at their homes instead. This was because, in the past, when the farmers sent it over to the warehouses, the warehouse people would sell their goods without agreement. Therefore, when the price increased, they didn't have the goods anymore, so the farmers lost a lot of money.

---

7 B2B is an abbreviation of the phrase "Business to Business." This is a form of business, trading between businesses.
8 B2C (Business-to-Consumer) means "Business to Customer" – a form of e-commerce transaction between a company and a consumer (customer).

Therefore, now the farmers only sell coffee at their own price. All traders who sold first had to buy back goods for delivery. This was the problem for the entire coffee export business system worldwide, the same struggle and difficulty, with huge losses.

I've been in the business for 18 years, but I'd never had to take control of management as arduously as this year. People usually ask me, "Which year was the most difficult to do business?" I always answer that every year is difficult, but no year is the same!

We were still inexperienced in the consumer business, so I had to outsource the consulting and other work. All those years of doing export business were not as painful as the past three years. At first, I hired a marketing staff member to work as a director. In B2B, normally, the owner would be the director. However, in B2C, I did not manage and operate the Company well enough. In my opinion, that was the reason why I failed and made mistakes. Everyone made promises, but it was a mess when they left, and we had to clean things up. When we looked at the ledgers, we saw huge losses. Yet, the most painful part was still to come.

At the end of 2018, we cleaned up after an employee left. A friend working with me in marketing introduced another person to become a director. At that time, I had done well at Phuc Sinh Corporation, but had too many responsibilities. I was not ready to run a consumer business. So, I agreed to hire him and he expected an over-the-top salary. He made a good sales commitment, but the revenue only reached 20 percent; the salary did not change. He left a lot of expired goods, and all the old backlogs were unresolved. Then he resigned because the revenue was insufficient to pay his salary.

We started investigating, and the more we uncovered, the more we felt cheated. We were scammed all the time, but we paid too much this time. We told him the company no longer had money to do business. Half a month's salary was left for him, but his mistakes were like he was cheating us. We had to try to sell goods to pay debts to suppliers and solve the backlog of distributors, agents, and customers.

I told him we were solving the problems so that we could pay him. However, he went and told his story about getting paid late to his friend, a journalist at a newspaper that knew nothing other than what he was telling them. We felt like a piece of meat between hyenas. They just posted without verification. We also discovered that he previously worked for another very large company in the consumer goods industry, where he also sold news to the press. That company did not fire him but moved him to another department, and eventually he had to leave. Before that horrifying incident, we thought he was a decent employee. He had such a history of lying and selling information from the company he was working for that no decent company would dare hire him.

After nearly four years of hiring CEOs and losing large amounts of money, I decided to run Phuc Sinh Consumer Corporation myself. I worked hard and picked up little by little, diligently convincing each customer, one by one, to buy a pack of coffee. After many years of hiring leadership for the company and receiving many complaints about customer service, I realize now the hired CEOs in this industry only care about themselves and "feed off" the company rather than tend to the customers.

Our coffee had also gradually become known to the public, perhaps thanks to our quality. A friend told me, "You may lose a lot, but you still get it; your coffee has good quality, so consumers still support you. You didn't know how to manage, so you didn't provide good customer service, but as long as you still have the quality, you still have customers. If you change to provide better service and pay more attention to customer service, I believe with product quality and design, even more customers will support you." I was tired and sad about the mess the previous directors left behind, but I suddenly felt much happier after hearing this.

I managed the company to focus on customer service, returning the goods and pursuing referrals. The sales came, and

I paid suppliers, dealers and distributors. In the end, the company solved all the outstanding problems. People believed and started ordering. We needed to make goods continuously for more than a month after I took charge.

After becoming the first company in Vietnam to produce freeze-dried green peppercorn, we introduced it to the local market. I first asked myself, "Why didn't we introduce freeze-dried peppercorn on our online purchasing page?" We have e-commerce at www.kphucsinh.vn, so we simultaneously introduced a range of peppercorns on our website, focusing on freeze-dried peppercorns. Everyone was very supportive. I felt sure that every market was fierce but also full of opportunities. If we provide good products, we always have support from customers.

Then the price of coffee went up, and the coffee crop came. A lot of coffee was bought and sold, everything was busy again. Most importantly, Phuc Sinh Consumer Corporation was no longer afraid of being scammed. Customers were very supportive. We felt so much happier and more confident. A new year was coming. Looking back, many things had happened this year; it was not an easy year for almost any company in the world. However, in bitterness, there was sweetness. If you do well and are persistent and creative, there will be many good people to support you. The good news was that a very large and reputable newspaper wanted to cover our story, even without asking anything from us! It is true that nice people meet nice people. At the end of the year: green peppercorn was produced, the website went live, and the factory was completed, the company was well managed, and a lot of other good news ... It was heartwarming. Hopefully, a new year will bring many new investment opportunities!

BUSINESS LAWSUIT

The cell phone rang.

"Hello, who's on the line?"

"Hi, David. It's Mai. I'm with Goldsmith GmbH; I've known you for a long time and have been following you on Facebook. I respect you a lot. Last time I went to Vietnam, I visited your company; but you were on a business trip, so I couldn't meet you."

"I know you, Mai; yet we haven't talked before. How long have you been with Goldsmith?"

"I was born in Da Nang. After completing my degree, I've always worked here. I've been working here for five years. I have something to discuss with you. Since you are the CEO, you will have a more multi-dimensional view. Why is it so difficult for me to work with Andrew? He is a bit rigid and just says no to everything, and to simply follow the contract."

"Yeah, I think he's very committed, so he could sometimes be a bit rigid. Just tell me the story."

"Yes, sir. Well, on our side, we buy a lot of goods and usually want to negotiate. I'm sure you understand. My company buys 20 containers a year. If the quality meets European standards, we won't complain. I hope you can stop this lawsuit. My boss wants to talk with you."

"Is that so? I called him a few times and sent him text messages. Now he insists on talking?"

"Yes, I'll convince him to call you. Could you let me know when it would be convenient for you?"

"Well, Wednesday evening. It will be easier to talk then."

"Well then, I wish you a nice evening and hope both sides can work this out."

The next morning, I went to the office. "Andrew, Mai called me yesterday."

"Mai from Goldsmith?"

"Yeah, she wants to convince me to stop this lawsuit. She said she'd tell Marco to call me and negotiate. They must have heard you say you were bringing the case to the London Arbitration Center, so they're nervous. Just give it a try," I remarked.

Andrew said, "Mai is very nice; whenever there are problems, she solves them."

"Oh, Andrew, please prepare a file for me, with a full contract for me to review, especially the transaction letters."

"When was the original contract signed?"

"September, and delivery from October to January next year."

"Why would you sign the contract for so long? How could you know the business situation?"

"This customer has been with us for a long time and is highly prestigious in the market; you also already agreed."

"Yeah, I was just saying that."

This year, Covid-19 has made everything difficult; it stopped everything. When Europe and the US experienced a lockdown, it was extremely difficult. Peppercorn prices fell dramatically and hit their lowest prices in the past ten years. We have been doing everything we can, but it is still difficult to thrive. Luckily, the customers who buy are very well-committed, especially in traditional markets such as Europe.

Wednesday night, my personal phone rang. "Hi, Marco. How are you?"

"Hi, David. I'm fine. Mai told me to call you."

"Yes, she also asked me to talk with you. So, how do you want to solve this?"

"We signed four contracts with you for US$3,800 per ton, and the quality you delivered was not good. We want to cancel all of them. I warned you many times, but you still delivered with such poor quality."

"Marco, our goods at the destination of Hamburg were all inspected and certified by GBA;[9] the quality is high in compliance with European standards."

---

9 GBA: name of the inspection company.

"I know, but it's not enough."

"What is not enough, sir? Can you tell me?"

"Our customers need better quality. This shipment does not meet the standard."

"Marco, look at the contract. It is stated that as long as the products meet the regulations on pesticide residues and circulation standards in Europe, it is fine."

"No, I repeat, we are asking for higher quality. However, we will accept the import if you reduce the price."

"How much do you want to reduce it by?"

"We want to reduce it by US$500 per ton."

"So we lose US$32,000? Not possible! I can only agree to reduce it by US$300 per ton."

"No. So we'll cancel the contract." That was the end of the call.

I called Andrew and said, "Marco wanted a reduction of US$500 per ton."

"Why so much? Have you decided?"

"I offered to reduce it by US$300 per ton, but he refused."

"How will we move forward? If things have gotten to this, what else can we do but sue? Just pay the London Arbitration Center."

"It's a lot, a few hundred million VND! And we don't know how things will turn out …"

"So? Just do it; let's see how it goes. When we take business to the world, we must show that we know how to do business!"

Andrew then wrote a letter to the client stating that we did not agree to the requested price reduction of US$500 per ton and have decided to sue the client through the IGPA London Arbitration Center.

Normally, Vietnamese people rarely do business abroad so intensely. I have never heard of lawsuits filed by Vietnamese businesses abroad, and even less about the results! Perhaps our company was quite different. We do a lot of overseas business. If we didn't sue fiercely, we wouldn't know who to rely on or trust to do business with. I also wanted to try it, just to be clear.

The customers didn't respond after receiving the letter. Perhaps they didn't think Vietnamese people were like that or weren't exactly used to that. How could a Vietnamese company sue a company in Europe?

Two days later, we received a letter confirming receipt of fees paid and a notice of an official case hearing from the London Arbitration Center. Mai also did not contact us. Maybe she was very sad. I had wanted to negotiate a good deal agreeable to us both, but there was nothing more I could do. Mai's boss, Marco, made this decision. I don't think she wanted her company to be sued, and I didn't want to sue them. I still wanted to come to a resolution. However, we could not accept being treated that way. For many years, we lost a lot of money shipping products to customers when we sold low and then the price increased. They could have asked for sympathy if they were in a difficult situation, but they had an arrogant and contemptuous attitude here. In the past, we had accepted to cancel contracts for customers in Hungary and Romania when they asked due to their difficulties. But this is the wealthiest market in Europe, and the customers were arrogant. I whispered, "Sorry, Mai. My company still has to sue your company."

The court hearing went very quickly. It took just one week for both sides to provide further evidence. Then each side defended themselves, and so on. At this point, I saw a problem with Goldsmith's counter argument. Marco wrote letters explaining things in a roundabout way. He begged, repeatedly asking for more time. None of the information Goldsmith gave was valid. The first arbitration verdict accepted my company's claims but forced Phuc Sinh to pay more money, up to several hundred million VND!

"Andrew, write to the Arbitration Center and ask why it is so much. We paid it last time as requested by them!" I told Andrew.

"For your company, this is the cost of the final verdict. We only pass a verdict when we receive enough money," the London Arbitration Center replied.

"Andrew, my answer is this: When Goldsmith loses, tell them to pay. Otherwise, the plaintiff will pay and collect from the defendant," I told him.

We had a meeting. If the court's decision is similar to the case in Romania and the customer cannot pay in case of losing, what could I do? Thinking and thinking.

We received a message from the London Arbitration Center again, asking us to pay by the next week in order to receive the verdict.

I was halfway there; was it time to stop? No. We decided to pay them.

We sent the money transfer Swift code[10] to the Arbitration Center, and the next day we got the verdict; amazing! Goldsmith customers must pay the full fee plus the current price difference. An unexpected number!

We shared the details with our partners, and they fully supported us. They said we had to do this to keep the business clean! But they also said the judgment was too weak! No punishment, no deterrence. However, we just hoped to get the money back. We didn't know how we could contact them, so our partner introduced us to one of their lawyers. That made us very happy.

We arranged contact with the attorneys, who were eager to help. We asked how much it would cost … At the same time, we wrote a formal letter to Goldsmith asking for enforcement of the judgment: "Transfer the money to us." We reminded them every week.

Two weeks later …

"Boss, this amount of money looks very strange, almost similar to the judgment of the London Arbitration Center," Andrew shouted.

"That's it. Check it out!"

---

10 Swift: wire transfer.

"That's right, boss!" Andrew replied.

So Goldsmith GmbH paid! They complied with the ruling. It was nice. Doing business with Europe is great; they are very law-abiding. We were happy, for many things: Getting reimbursed for the fees we paid, receiving the price difference and especially the fact that our reputation in the European market had increased significantly. This year, the Covid-19 pandemic occurred, but it was also the year that we received money from distant customers that seemed impossible to retrieve. This made us continue to uphold our business and human beliefs.

Ho Chi Minh City, January 2, 2021.

HAPPY LIFE

There are many gods living among us. If there is a god of happiness, there will be a god of unhappiness; if there is a god of luckiness, there will be a god of unluckiness. If there is a god of Complaint and irritability, there will be a god of Silence and wellness ... If you want a particular god to come to you, create an environment suitable for them to come and live with you.

To live a happy life, you must create a happy environment so the god of happiness can visit you. When you express your happiness and kindness, the god of happiness will visit you more. Your life will always be happy.

In contrast, the god of irritability will inevitably come if you are irritable. As long as you are irritable, that god will always be with you. You will always feel frustrated and uncomfortable.

Regardless of your social status, being visited by the gods is your choice: the gods of happiness and luckiness, or the gods of unhappiness and complaint; it all depends on your spirit and your life choices. You can find a way to always be happy. You'll surely be happy when you choose K HAPPY LIFE – Drink toward a Happy Life!

With K HAPPY LIFE, you are completely refreshed! K Coffee's HAPPY LIFE has a sophisticated design, an elegant aesthetic and top quality that will satisfy you and even the most demanding people. K HAPPY LIFE makes you smile and laugh with everyone. It relieves any invisible pressures. The God of Joy and Happiness will be with you forever with K HAPPY LIFE ...

What are you waiting for? Get some K HAPPY LIFE Coffee to bring you the God of Happiness, leading to a HAPPY LIFE, a true life.

ASSOCIATION

She looked through the window; it was sunny with very little wind. This day was her last day at the office. "Tomorrow is the day of my retirement," she said joyfully. After over 30 years of working in a state institute, everything had finally ended. She felt happier thinking of having more time to visit her two children in Australia. Yet, when she arrived home, everything felt so sluggish. She just wanted to lie in bed and rest.

"Why are you laying in the dark?" her husband came and asked.

"What time is it?"

"It's 7.15 p.m."

"Yeah, I don't know why I laid down for so long. I just fell asleep, I guess. I'll get up and see if there's anything to cook, then we'll have dinner."

When she woke the following morning, she still felt quite tired. Before she retired, she had been thinking about what she would do when the day came.

A month ago, an association of agricultural products called her to ask if she wanted to work for them. At that time, she didn't want to answer. It had been years of working for the government with a stagnant mindset. Working by mainly relying on relationships, not her ability, made her tired and scared. She asked them to let her think about it, though she had never considered taking the position.

After breakfast, her phone vibrated. There was a middle-aged man's voice on the other end. "Ms. Thu? I'm Trong from Association N. We heard through Mr. T of the Ministry of Agriculture that you had just retired, so I called you. The Association needs to fill the position of General Secretary, and we'd like to invite you to take the position. What do you think?"

With the accumulated wisdom of working in a government position for over 30 years, she replied she would consider the offer. She asked him to give her two weeks to respond.

After finishing the things that needed to be done in the morning, it was already 10:30 a.m. She suddenly saw a bag of coffee that her brother in the industry told her was from an acquaintance and was really good, so she tried it. Opening a packet of filtered coffee, she sat at a table outside in the courtyard. She drank it and started thinking. First, she had to visit her daughters in Australia to see how they were. The idea of being able to visit her children without having to worry about work made her really happy. Her two children loved her very much, often sharing their lives and jobs with her. Their mother-daughter relationships were close. The visa and plane tickets were all completed. In two days, she would be able to see her children.

Welcoming her at the airport was her foreign son-in-law and eldest daughter. She felt very relieved and happy. On the way home, the three of them talked in both English and Vietnamese. She also spent time studying abroad, so her English was good. Her son-in-law could follow the conversation and didn't need to ask: "What did your parents say?" like she often saw other western grooms ask.

Her daughter only had weekends off and then had to go to work. The grandchildren played with her and went to school. She stayed at home to clean and cook for them. The first two days were fun, but she felt homesick on the third day, missing her husband. He was always interested in asking her questions, so she turned on Viber and spoke with him.

"Today, I went to the center and happened to meet some of your colleagues. While talking with them, they asked me if you were working for the N Association. I said you hadn't decided yet."

"Oh, I forgot. I have to answer them soon."

"Just relax for ten days. When you come back, you can think about answering them."

In her free time, she watched TV and read some books. However, in Australia, everything was empty and different from Vietnam. Two days before returning home, she thought about what she would do in Vietnam. She worked a lot and always met up with a lot of friends. If she stayed home for a long time, she might not like it very much. It was soon time to return to Vietnam, and her husband was happy to welcome her home.

"Maybe I'll go see what the Association is like, and maybe I'll work there," she said.

"Yes, just do what you like and have fun," her husband replied.

Time flew by quickly, and she had been working for the Association for two months. The Association's activities were simpler than before. She had meetings with different companies, including state-owned, foreign, and private. Among them, she noticed the Hanh Phuc Company. The name sounded strange, and it seemed that the owner was smart. With many years of experience in the state, she was a bit wary of the owner. It was only natural, but it didn't mean anything. The previous manager of her position praised him; she was glad she could see for herself. During meetings, he always gave very frank and knowledgeable opinions. She thought his company was the number one exporter! Well, privately owned *and* the number one exporter, both domestically and internationally, it is really respectable. Moreover, everyone in her family worked in the private sector or foreign companies, so she had a reasonably fair view.

The Association was to organize the International Spice Conference. Lots of foreign guests would come, but the budget was small. She thought the reception should also be quite decent. Other countries had organized it well in the past. If Vietnam does not organize well enough, it would be really embarrassing for guests. So, she asked the companies in the Executive Committee to sponsor the Association in holding the conference. The atmosphere was stiff, but after a while, the Director of Hanh Phuc Company said that his company would sponsor them with 100 million VND. Then, the atmosphere seemed to be more pleasant. Other companies agreed to sponsor varying amounts of between 5 and 20 million VND, which was enough to organize the conference and have a decent reception; it was much less worrisome.

After a few instances like that, she felt that the young Director of the Hanh Phuc Company did not seem so self-interested; he only gave suggestions for sponsorship. Gradually she came to understand him more. "I'm probably too defensive," she thought.

At a meeting of the Executive Committee of the Association, people were airing their points of view. When it was time for him to speak, the Director of Hanh Phuc Company stood up.

"Minh, do you have an opinion?"

"Yes. I think we have to change, guys! Instead of waiting for companies to come to Vietnam to buy goods, we should take goods to introduce abroad at exhibitions."

The entire room was silent; no one said anything. Passive thinking left them speechless.

"My company has been doing this for decades, and this is how we changed," Minh added.

Finally, the Chairman of the Association said, "I think we need to stay vigilant and think carefully and seriously before deciding!"

"You should think about what I said. I will give you a contact address for a foreign exhibition organization. It's very good; I will let my manager come as a guide," Minh told Ms. Thu after the meeting.

Two weeks later, she contacted the foreign exhibition organization and was completely convinced that attending the exhibition was ideal and constructive. It would create many opportunities for businesses. When she presented it to the Association President, he said, "I don't like us going to the fair. Plus, Minh is too young to give such an opinion."

"Minh, the Chairman did not agree to go to the fair," Ms. Thu informed him.

The following year, the meeting of the Executive Committee with the Association's members came as scheduled.

Minh commented again, and this time everyone seemed to agree. After a period of going to the fair, the companies seemed to be satisfied. Their direct sales increased significantly, and there were more knowledgeable customers. The members stated that next time they wouldn't need sponsors as they would pay for themselves. A good idea took almost two years to be understood and implemented in the digital internet age!

At the summary meeting, everyone said that Minh was so good and that the fair was very good. The Chairman said, "We knew this even before Hanh Phuc Company; we went to the fair a long time ago." A silence followed this.

Then someone said: "No, the idea about the fair came from Minh and Hanh Phuc Company!" Nobody said anything more; everyone just smiled at each other.

Meeting with the Executive Committee again, Minh said, "We have to reform and we have to change!" Everyone was rushing to say yes, reform and elect a new President.

"Why change? We are doing well. I still want to be President!" the current President said.

"You've been in this position for 14 to 15 years. Almost since the Association was established ..."

Opinions were mixed. Someone said, "If it's good, why should we change; I still feel good."

All the disagreements made Ms. Thu feel tired. She thought it looked exactly like a scene from the decades of working at the governmental institute!

Suddenly, a voice interrupted her thoughts. "What do you think if we elect you as President?"

"Oh, no, I won't do it. I have other plans," Thu replied.

"You mustn't have any plans to quit!" Minh said.

"No, I won't quit. I'll continue working."

"Perhaps instead of just the large member companies participating in the fair, why doesn't the Association organize all the formalities and then register the smaller company members also? Thus saving everyone time and effort. Small companies would have better conditions and more opportunities," Minh suggested.

So the small companies signed up immediately and had their booth at one of the biggest fairs in the middle of Europe for very cheap fees. After seeing smaller companies sign up, one or two big companies also wanted to join, but there were no available spaces.

"Leave small companies out to make room for bigger companies," the Chairman told her.

"I can't; we have to be transparent. We called to encourage them to participate in the fair and pay, and they paid immediately."

"It was too much," she thought. "If things are unfair, no one will join next time."

She was feeling very frustrated when she received a phone call from Minh. "I just went to a spice conference, and they had a very good product introduction video. Why don't we do that?"

"It's too expensive!"

"Hanh Phuc Company will sponsor you."

"But I see that all the Presidents, Vice Presidents or promoters in Asia know English, and they all speak English at the conference; only Vietnam does not …"

"Mr. Chairman, Minh's friend said that making a video would be good and easy. He recommended ASM to me. They would sponsor 70 percent of the video, and Hanh Phuc would sponsor 30 percent. Should we do it?"

"Do nothing! Minh is still very young; why does he keep talking so much?"

"He's not that young, almost 40 years old, and it's because they're enthusiastic for the Association. Hanh Phuc Company would make no profit here."

"I said no. Let me tell you that the other Associations did worse and were not financially clear. Every time, they spend a few billion VND without consulting with the Executive Committee members. I am the Vice President of that Association, and they didn't even ask me. They spend the funds without talking to or requesting the consent of the Vice President. I might think it was their backyard! We stop here."

"After years of working at the governmental institute, I have encountered so many slimy scenes. I wonder why they work at the Association without devoting themselves, trying to gather power and smother those with good ideas?" That thought made her tear up.

Minh met the members of the Association again, and one of them said that he didn't need English to do business, sell goods and many other things!

"Yes," Minh replied, realizing he was talking about the members representing the Association who knew English. They must have noticed what Minh said at that time.

After seven years working with the Association, many things had happened; Minh felt he did not have any allies or partners to share with. While he was thinking, the company Director walked in.

"If you keep sharing the company's business secrets, it will become difficult for us," the Director told Minh.

"If you work for the Association, you should help support and share the work with the Association. To let the small businesses join the Association and have better business opportunities to connect. It's not just for the chair, the reputation and a few million VND monthly salary; I don't do things like that. As a private person, I'm not used to going to the Association to listen and keep quiet. Life goes by so fast; I'm almost 50 years old, thank you," Minh replied.

The Director went out, and Minh sat alone in a large room and thought: "I've worked enthusiastically with no allies. The opinions I've given were either beaten down or rejected. If they did use my idea, they would say bad things behind my back. What am I dedicating myself to? On the surface, it's friendly. But there are many evil intentions hidden." Minh wondered, "What does the Association do?" More than ever, he understood Thu's disengaged feeling.

Suddenly, a resignation letter popped into his mind. Minh looked out the skylight in Saigon, and the season's first rain started. The rain washed away all the dirt and made the air cleaner.

BUSINESS TRIP

It's a snowy day. Gershion looks out the window, and everything is quiet. Today, he has a meeting with a company that supplies goods from Vietnam. Normally, they visit his office and company every year in January when the weather is very cold and snowy. He also adored this young man, who was always cheerful and pleasant. While he was thinking this, his secretary entered his office with his guest from Vietnam.

"Hi, Minh. How are you? Did you enjoy the flight?"

"Hello, Gershion. Everything is fine; the flight was quite smooth."

In the meeting, he usually asked many questions about Vietnam's crops, inventories, speculative storage, quality, etc. Gershion said that many companies offered products from Vietnam in recent years, and many startups offered very competitive prices. "Minh, if you want to survive, you need to work harder," Gershion said.

Minh would travel from Vietnam and visit customers every year. Happy Spice is a company that Minh has known and sold pepper and other Spices to for a long time, over ten years. Every year in January, before the harvest, Minh flies to the US to see them. The owner of Happy Spice is a Jewish man named Gershion. He is very competent and strong. Gershion is proud to be an American even though he was born in Romania and crossed the border to Italy at the age of 19. He then came to the US empty-handed with his brother. The two brothers did all sorts of things to survive and then joined a large spice factory as staff. When the two brothers were over 40, they left the factory and started their own business. They opened their own spice factory named Happy Spice. The company is now over 30 years old and has hundreds of employees.

Every year, Minh suspects something is wrong. Recently, the amount of goods Minh sold to this customer had decreased significantly. Minh was looking to find out the reason for this.

Gershion said, "The only reason is the price, Minh. You always quote higher prices than others, and we also need a good price to sell to our customers. Your prices are not competitive; we can't buy at those prices."

The meeting continued, and Minh thought, "I must find a way." During the meeting, Minh felt that Mr. Gershion seemed to have slowed down and become more contemplative. Although he was 80 years old, Mr. Gershion still worked hard and went on business trips, which he must do to continue learning. In Vietnam, Minh's friends always set the milestone of retiring by 45 or 50 years old. But every time he traveled out of Vietnam, he would see 70- and 80-year-old customers who were still working very hard. At the end of the meeting, Gershion spoke to Minh before going to lunch. Looking at Mr. Gershion, Minh knew that this man had been running his business for over 40 years and went on annual business trips. He goes to Vietnam every two years but has always been careful in trading agricultural products due to drastic price fluctuations. Recently his life had been disturbed, as his wife had died. But one thing that surprised Minh was that when he saw him to the door, Mr. Gershion stopped and spoke to Minh very naturally.

"Minh, I must share this with you: My wife passed away six months ago, and I have been searching but have not met a new companion. I have a house to take care of and many things to arrange by myself. I need a girlfriend to share these duties with me. You know what? I spent the last week in New York. I met with four women, and none pleased me. Some are too cold, some are too pushy, and some talk too much. I don't know what to do ..."

"Oh my gosh, how is an 80-year-old man so comfortable with such a topic?" Minh thought.

"Do you know that I've met dozens of women, some of whom have a whole family, a dead husband and six children? Some are widowed and bombard me relentlessly when we sit and talk. They do most of the talking, continuously for an hour. There are so many things I don't understand, and each woman is so different. If we must accept certain aspects of each other, I cannot make it work out!"

Minh was so shocked. How can you ask for an angel at this age? They must have a past and a bunch of descendants; how can they be lonely? But he still replied to Gershion, "Don't ask for much; just accept it!"

Seeing an 80-year-old man full of spirit getting to know these women, Minh was very curious and excited. He asked Gershion's daughter about the story. She happily replied that her father always took the time to meet these women. "He was in New York all week to get to know his potential girlfriend, and just got back yesterday," his daughter said.

Looking at this 80-year-old man looking for a girlfriend so enthusiastically, to see how he so openly shared the story with him, Minh found it extremely humorous. Why were Americans so different from us? Sometimes the excitement of reconnecting doesn't come from work, but from something very human.

"Visiting customers gives such advantages: building a close relationship and gaining a more realistic view, understanding how much more effort is needed to communicate," Minh thought.

Minh went to Florida to attend the American Spice Conference and met Gershion again the following April. Together, they ate grilled chicken skewers and talked. Gershion told Minh that finding a girlfriend was difficult, but he would not give up. He had just spent three days trying to figure things out with someone, but with no success. He knew Ann, his late wife, was awesome and found it hard! She was amazing, but he shouldn't compare others to her.

"It's not fair to compare others to a previous marriage. You were together for a long time, and you knew a lot (if not all) of her attributes. It's impossible to understand someone you have only known for a week or a month," Minh advised him. The old man smiled in agreement.

Minh thought about how American culture was so different from Vietnamese. "They have legitimate needs, and their personalities are very natural. The children and society support themselves strongly." But he wished basic issues were also supported.

"When you go to another country, the business is different, but the main difference is in the culture. These deeper things give us understanding and make us more generous with ourselves and those around us. Single parents and widowed parents, if you have the opportunity to find your other half to take care of and love each other, why don't you search boldly for them! It is certain that there is always more to life to share," Minh thought.

Every year, Minh goes on business trips and has many customers from around the world come to Ho Chi Minh City to visit him. The city is sunny and rainy all year round. Many friends like it when they visit. Others may complain about the heat and the noise. But after a few months or years living here, they like it, with the spirit of openness and freedom, where no one is too competitive. There is a strong spirit of freedom and entrepreneurship in each person. Evaluating one's surroundings requires better understanding, and shouldn't be hurried. "Sometimes hate could turn to love; you never know!" Minh said to himself.

Life just goes on. Today was the day Minh was about to leave for the US, not in the cold of January, but in April.

"Hi, Minh. Gershion wants to meet and discuss business with you. Can you meet with him in 30 minutes?" his secretary talked to Minh.

Minh checked his schedule and was almost fully booked. "Or invite him to lunch?" Minh replied.

Five minutes later: "Okay, Minh. Let's have lunch."

As soon as the previous meeting ended, he was walking out of the main hotel lobby when Gershion arrived.

"Hello, Minh. How are you today?"

"Hi, Gershion. Everything is fine."

"Minh, I'm married!" the old man excitedly shared everything.

An old man over 80 constantly sought a partner after his previous wife passed away. His excitement in sharing this made Minh both happy and no-less amused than the first time he heard it. Three times he had gone to the US to meet customers, and three times the old man shared the exciting stories of looking for a wife. After the good news, both had successful negotiations.

Today was Minh's last meeting in the cold and windy city of Chicago, and tomorrow, he would fly home. There are always good experiences on every trip. Minh felt closer to his family and company every morning. Perhaps that is the best thing after every trip.

VIETNAMESE WOMEN
DEDICATED TO VIETNAMESE WOMEN

Mom

My mother gave birth to nine children, two of them passed away when they were young and raised seven to adulthood. From a young age, my mother and siblings worked until late at night, sometimes until 1 a.m., then woke up at 5 a.m. to cook rice and bran, and do everything else. Parents raised their children to grow up and take care of their studies. It was so tough, yet mothers would not complain. Hardship seemed to become easier on my mother's hands. My mother was well organized and managed to provide rice and clothes for us. Through the most difficult years, my mom always considered such obstacles typical and always overcame them. She sold any product she could have thought of to earn money to support the family; eating alone was extremely rare for a family comprising grandma, parents and seven children. There were years of rice mixed with starch. Even though the cast-iron pot was full, with ten people eating, the rice would be quickly devoured. Sitting by the pot were my mother and elder sisters, taking turns handing the remaining seven people rice. In the family, it is no surprise that a mother makes sacrifices for her children. Perhaps I was too young at the time to realize it.

Although the situation was difficult, my parents always encouraged us to study hard. As a result, five children in a row went to university. My parents were very patient because those who failed the exam were allowed to retake it. One of my sisters took the exam three times in order to get accepted by a university.

After finishing university, it was difficult to get a job during the subsidy period. At that time, Vietnam had not opened its economy. My mother was always the one who looked for jobs for my brothers and sisters. She always built relationships in order to help them find a job. Sometimes, she asked people for years, and they always promised, but never took action. I had always seen her persistently try to earn a living to support us, but she was sometimes meek when looking for jobs for my sisters. My mother did everything without fearing hardship as long as it was good for her children.

An unforgettable memory:

"Mom is back! Were you able to find a job for sister? Will she be accepted?" I asked my mom.

"The Director of the Paper Company absolutely refused to take gifts. Whatever I said, he denied! I was tired of sitting there for an hour trying to persuade him, but he firmly refused."

"He's so stubborn. I really wonder if she can get the job ..."

I saw my mother's fatigue and shame. I loved her very much but didn't know what to do because I was young.

When I went to school, my parents did everything for me to have a life like everyone else. But, at that time, my parents were both retired. Their effort was quite considerable!

When I graduated, I applied for a job and managed my life independently. I always tried my best, so my parents wouldn't have to worry too much about me.

Wife

We got married three months after I started my own company. Generally speaking, we were poor. My family was in Hai Phong city, and we lived in Saigon city. After we married, my wife stayed home for over four years to raise the children. When the factory started its operation, my wife said she wanted to go to work, and she prepared for it. She learned everything quickly, patiently humbling herself and swallowing her ego well. Purchasing was difficult in the agricultural industry, especially the raw material industry. She learned everything in order to be able to buy goods and perform as well as purchasing managers in other multinational companies and the largest companies in Vietnam at that time.

After that, we built houses and factories continuously. My wife learned about construction and architecture very quickly. She supervised the construction of many houses and factories and gave very effective design ideas. Once, when we were building our house, a neighbor saw my wife coming to supervise. He ran over and said, "Where is your husband? Why would he let you do so much?"

My wife laughed and said, "In a family, one person must be in charge of making money and one person spending money. My husband works to earn money so I can spend money to buy and build a house."

Vietnamese women are like that; they are hardworking, resilient, patient, and respected.

Friends in the Industry

I manage nine directors in the company. They are factory managers and office representatives, seven of which are female. Doing recruitment, I always thought that men would have an advantage over women. After working in an environment full of women, I realized women are far superior. Men are often narcissistic and consider themselves the most important. They do not want to do small things, just the big things. They give up easily when working, while women persist in both small and big things. These days, you will mainly see women in the workforce; women are often the main earners for the family.

I have foreign friends who are chief representatives of offices or general directors of companies in Vietnam; sometimes we would meet up for coffee or drinks together.

"Quang, Vietnamese women are good; they are patient and fulfill tasks well. But why are the men so weak? Even narcissistic and give up easily?" said my foreign friend.

I responded, "I don't know. I went home and tried to find an explanation because I have experienced these problems myself when recruiting or working with certain people.

Huge Raw Agricultural Material Industry

The export revenue of peppercorn is about one billion dollars. Coffee earns over three billion dollars, and cashew nuts over two billion dollars, among many other products. From the plains to the highlands, the women control business decisions. The male employees drive cars to collect money and inspect and deliver goods.

In foreign companies and foreign representative offices in Vietnam, chief representatives, decision-makers, and purchasing directors are mostly female. Very few males. Why is that?

From a world perspective, in Europe, America and the rest of Asia: purchasing managers, general managers and other managers are predominantly males. But it is the complete opposite in Vietnam. How can this be explained?

After working in Vietnam for a while, I've met many foreigners who have asked me, "Why are Vietnamese women so talented and strong?" I have tried to find the answer, but I am not convinced by my own conclusions.

The eldest female sibling in the family often has to work as her mother does, especially in the countryside of Vietnam. The first and second sisters are usually very brave. As for a son, he is often much more spoiled, so men's integration to society, or more specifically, to work, is much slower.

Society

I have a friend who has a fairly successful family business. One day, while drinking a glass of beer, he said he had to go on business trips for five to six months out of the year. He finally told his wife:

"I'm too tired to go. I don't know if I can go again."

"Don't be arrogant!" his wife said. "Now, people want to be busy but can't! If you're tired, just take a few days off. The family and I will take care of you. When you aren't tired anymore, you can continue to work. When we are still young, we have to work hard. We won't be able to do anything when we're old and weak, even if we wanted to!"

After his wife said that, how could he be lazy? He must continue to work hard again.

I have this female friend who really supported my writing. Whenever I go on a business trip, I often write about it to share with my colleagues. This way, they know about the cities that I go to and would have some general ideas when they go there themselves, allowing them to work more easily. Once she read my article, she enthusiastically encouraged me to continue writing. She said I am gifted at writing and that she would help with the editing process. Thus, my articles were born. Without her encouragement, I wouldn't have written and been featured in newspapers. Both children and adults in life and work need encouragement to develop their abilities. I was emboldened to write, and I am grateful for this.

Writing is also great because it relieves stress and often leads to self-discovery. There are many things that I didn't know I could do if I hadn't discovered them myself. For me, writing is a journey of self-awareness. Life is like a rope with many knots, and it's great that at each stage you discover the ability to do that for yourself. As I untie one or more knots, I find myself better skilled and able to do this or that. The deeper life gets explored, the more color we get.

I have a friend who sells paintings and has built a large gallery for herself. She flies to many places and explores the world. Multiple five-star hotels in Saigon are decorated with paintings by artists she is either exclusively or mainly representing. She takes great pride when decorating such notable hotels as the Park Hyatt, Sheraton, Intercontinental and others …

When a family is in financial difficulty, we always see the wife and mother struggling to work. Regardless of how difficult it is, they'll earn money to support the family. But men are rarely seen doing this.

When I go to other countries, I see women do not have to struggle so hard. In Korea and Japan, this is obvious. It is also obvious in countries and regions such as Singapore, Hong Kong, Indonesia or Taiwan, where men are the key people in families who struggle to earn money. I went to a market in Budapest, Hungary, similar to Ben Thanh market in Vietnam. I primarily saw men working. Women were rarely seen as vendors, from selling fish to vegetables, fruits or children's toys.

One day, I went out for a run in the morning. I smelled fried eggs and bread from afar. When I approached, I saw a man riding a motorbike with a creatively installed rear glass cage with bread and an egg fryer. Naturally, I was glad to see men driving around and doing this because mostly women have been doing it in this area. At the street markets, it is found that men are more involved in trading in the South than the North, although not much compared to other regions in the world.

Once, I went to say goodbye to a customer who had been in Vietnam for ten days for a survey. Since I had left early, we had a few minutes to drink coffee. He said: "I am surprised that Vietnamese women are both beautiful and talented, seeing that men always make tea and women always control the business." I just laughed and didn't know what to say.

On the Sidelines of Women's Stories

I am a CEO of an agricultural product company. After many years, I have noticed that when negotiating with female partners; I am not as persistent and intense as when working with foreign male bosses or colleagues. I didn't mean to adjust my behavior as I wasn't aware of this; I analyzed the logic to find the answer. Perhaps it is unconscious because I respect them. My actions are somewhat humble and not as fierce or drastic as with male partners outside of Vietnam.

Vietnamese women tend to do everything, from financing for the family to building relations with the local government where they live, or searching suitable schools for their children and teaching them ... I am aware of this constantly after many years of observing. My mother worked very hard; therefore, I had to be in charge to reduce the burden on my family. I always attend parent conferences, apply to schools for my children, and patiently teach them.

One afternoon, while drinking tea, my wife said, "In novels, I see stories about filial piety, but with what I've witnessed in real life, I have seen no one more filial than you. I just hope our eldest son is as filial as you are or close to it; then I will be satisfied." I looked at my wife and saw how wonderful life was. And you, if you've read what I've written, what do you think?

Ho Chi Minh City, on the evening of July 6, 2017.

I GO RETAILING

Vietnam has hundreds of thousands of coffee shops, but it is hard to find any direct supplying consumers with unroasted green coffee beans.

It is normally not possible to find shops that sell such items. I want to buy it but don't know where to get it.

Green bean coffee (also known as green coffee beans) is a rare commodity that is sold directly to people for self-roasting, ensuring pure and natural coffee for health and food safety.

Coffee is the third-most globally consumed commodity after rice and flour, meaning we consume it daily. Some people drink three to four cups of coffee daily; others may drink only one cup. Finding shops selling rice is easy, all over from the street markets to the supermarket; also, if you want to make bread, you can buy flour. Although it may be more difficult than rice, it's still easy to find. Yet, there is almost nowhere to buy green coffee beans for roasting. I have rarely seen a shop that sells green coffee beans to coffee shops that want to roast, or household mills that want to buy green coffee to roast.

Therefore, the input for coffee shops is roasted beans and ground coffee. Direct traceability is difficult. Consumers always ask: "What's in those coffee skins? Soybeans, corn, chemicals or flavorings?" The question always exists, but the answer is always unclear.

Meanwhile, in countries that consume a lot of coffee, such as Belgium, the Netherlands, Germany and others; they always have shops selling green coffee to consumers. Coffee shops roast their green coffee beans. Small roasting businesses can purchase green coffee beans and roast the coffee if needed. For households who also want to roast green coffee beans for themselves, they possess their own coffee roasters. In countries such as Singapore and Hong Kong … many large coffee trading companies have opened stalls selling each bag of raw materials of green coffee beans to individuals and companies who want to roast coffee. However, in Vietnam, it is still rare to see this.

Many foreign customers who visit Vietnam would like to tour to see the raw materials of green coffee shops. Sadly, there are none. We can't find them, or they're hidden somewhere difficult to find. Another question is why Phuc Sinh does not supply the Vietnamese market with raw materials for green coffee beans. For nearly 20 years, we have been the supplier of green coffee beans for large enterprises and roasting companies of small and medium scale globally. During that 20 years, we have exported around 70,000 tons of coffee annually to many countries. The selection of high-quality raw green coffee bean products is very accessible to us.

Accordingly, in 2021, Phuc Sinh Corporation officially launched a series of green coffee products. Unroasted green coffee products such as Blue Son La, Super Clean Robusta, Blue Tiger, and Super Berry ... are packed in packages of 5kg, 10kg, and many other weights. This makes it convenient for customers who want to roast and grind their own coffee, which satisfies their needs.

Being in the top five largest coffee exporting companies in Vietnam and the leading Robusta exporter in the world, Phuc Sinh has fulfilled its mission to be a supplier and distributor of high-quality products. Green coffee products are of the highest quality and the most delicious, bringing premium quality coffee beans from farm to cup.

AN AMERICAN TRIP

Four years later, America had another presidential election. Except for Covid-19 and the wait for a new presidential term, everything in the US seems unchanged …

As usual, I tried to meet American clients at the beginning of the year. First, the US is the largest market for commodities, including peppercorn and coffee; and second, meeting customers at the beginning of the year gives me a new feeling – a very "fresh" one.

Nowadays, it is not difficult to enter the US!

I scheduled a meeting with a client and left for the United States. My family was preparing for the end of the year and the traditional Tet holiday in Vietnam. I still remember three years ago when I wrote about my trip to the US. I was frustrated waiting over three hours at the airport for immigration procedures. Due to the US government cutting staff, there were more than 24 counters then, but only nine were open, and progress was very slow. I said I didn't want to go to America anymore. Last year, the immigration procedure in the US was less than five minutes. Gosh! Quite a big change.

And this year, 2017, I entered the queue. After looking at my visa and passport, they guided me through the procedure with a scanner. There was someone to help, and without them asking me anything, I entered the country two minutes later. That's America … I always feel the spin, the drastic changes there.

After completing the procedure, I was excited to catch a taxi. It was quite cold that day, -6°C. I waited in line for a taxi to the hotel. New York has a lot of taxis, but golden airport taxis are the most trusted. Uber is also very convenient there and cheap too, only 75 percent of the price of a taxi. In New York, Uber does not expect a tip, but if you take a taxi, keep in mind that it costs a US$10 tip from the airport to a hotel in Manhattan.

A Different Business Culture

On my first day in the US, I visited clients in New York and New Jersey. All meetings must be scheduled in advance. Usually, when customers come to Vietnam, we pick them up at the airport and send a car to pick them up at the hotel. In the US, New York and New Jersey are very large. We have to take the initiative regarding transportation. We must "book" (register for) each meeting. When working with American customers, they are not too gracious and welcoming. They talk moderately, and no one offers water or coffee to their guests, even if they travel from far away. American businesses that work mainly in the US, having done little work in Asia, show their working style more clearly by not offering water while talking for one or two hours.

My general feeling is that customers in New York and New Jersey are anxious this year. They have a new President, and people don't yet know what direction life is going to take. A commodity dealer in the US, while having breakfast and drinking coffee, said very specifically, "I'm very worried and don't know what the economy will be like, how the policies will change …"

Aside from not being offered a glass of water or coffee in a conversational style when meeting customers, unlike in Vietnam, 100 percent of American customers praised the quality of Phuc Sinh's goods. Phuc Sinh's American Standard Goods (Asta) have had stable quality and good prices for the past year, so buying from Phuc Sinh is smart. The goods are guaranteed to be delivered, allowing customers not to worry. They can sleep very well. Life is very fun when we visit and are told so by customers.

In America, there are so many cultures and so many people. One of the biggest differences is that people often ask each other: "Where are you from?" In Vietnam, it is rare for someone to ask where you are from, even in Ho Chi Minh City, where millions of immigrants live and work.

The next day I flew to Omaha. As a small city, there is no direct flight from New York, so one must be in transit. In the US, it's normal to fly in transit, and it's also normal to be delayed. I woke up early and took two flights to meet customers. The weather was bone-chilling. Even though I was dressed warmly, it felt freezing cold while walking. We arrived early, so we went to town for lunch and were delighted to see a Vietnamese restaurant. I always eat Pho and also spring rolls. However, the pho had a different taste from my hometown and was served by Mexicans and white people. It was still fun to eat at a Vietnamese restaurant. Then we met the customer. We had to wait, with no coffee either!

In fact, large American companies all have self-service coffee shops. If they offer coffee, the staff or boss will have to serve you coffee themselves. Therefore, they rarely offer anything. I still remember five years ago, I sold a lot of coffee to customers in Hawaii. I flew from Vietnam to Hawaii, with a total transit time of nearly 30 hours. We met for 15 minutes, but on the way back, they placed 35 contracts. I talked about this with a loyal customer in Germany, and they said, "Oh Quang, not bad! You're there to sell goods, right? That's American culture, folks!"

I remember one time a Canadian customer talked about culture shock and said that a Hungarian customer must have felt abandoned when he first opened his door to the US to visit the market. In fact, it's not that Americans are cold or inhospitable to their partners; it's just these cultural differences. Regarding cultural differences: Canada and the US are geographically close, but the culture and behavior in business is extremely different. Canadians are very warm. I remember visiting clients in Canada for five days; I was constantly invited to such sumptuous lunches and dinners that I wished I could avoid the last dinner with them. America is different: there is no dinner. In Ohama, after meeting a client, we had dinner together, but the payment was made by my representative in the US, not the partners I met.

I still think for a business to be successful, you must understand your partner's business culture. I still remember my first time in Europe and my first time in Spain. The dinner time started at 10 p.m.! I was very surprised. Even in Europe, we see a big difference between Southerners and Northerners. For example, in Western Europe, such as the Netherlands, Germany and Switzerland, no one picks you up when you arrive. You do everything by yourself and schedule self-visits very similar to the US. Customers in Southern Europe, Spain, Italy and southern France will pick you up at the airport and invite you to dinner. They will send a car to pick you up and bring you to the office to meet them. The Netherlands, Belgium or France invite you to have a meal. Switzerland and Germany do not. It seems only the companies that come to Asia often have the habit of inviting guests to lunch and dinner.

Between the former West and East Germany, even the same country behaved with different business cultures. East German people were quite affectionate and warm, like the Vietnamese. They picked their partners up at the airport and even took them to their home to sleep. Lunch and dinner, they would pay. However, when they did business, they differed from West German people, which was slower. The confirmations could be canceled, and sometimes only from their side. Nonetheless, they did things quickly, which was almost always unchanged when confirmed. After many years of harmony, the difference in the behavior of the two regions was still very clear, even though East Germans went to West Germany to work quite a lot and East German cities became much busier.

Back to the trip: I flew to Milwaukee, and they offered me a bottle of water at the start of the meeting. Everyone thinks that Americans or Westerners generally have to travel a lot. Yet what I see here with managers of the big companies I meet, they have never been outside the United States. Some have never even left the city they live in. It's strange, isn't it? So I mainly try to understand their culture and don't expect them to understand Asian culture. After the meeting, we went out to find a Vietnamese restaurant while waiting for my flight to meet the next customer. The cold weather, the time difference and the unsuitable food all make me feel like I'm ... "frozen."

Leaving Wisconsin, we flew to Los Angeles. I flew a long time and arrived at the hotel at 11 p.m. Meeting guests and flying for 21 hours straight was difficult for me.

It is true that if you want to work hard, you need to be healthy. Working in the US is a challenge if you do not have good health and an open mind. Apart from the different cultures, you must always maintain a cheerful spirit while chatting and greeting customers. This may seem simple, but to do it continuously for so many days, by flying halfway around the world and then flying many times domestically to meet each customer while no one offers you a glass of water ... it's really not easy!

I visited Los Angeles for the third time and spent over a day touring the city. Los Angeles is big. My friend took me to the beach. To be honest, I haven't seen anything special since I arrived in Los Angeles, even after walking for half a day on Manhattan Beach. Housing here is said to be extremely expensive, more than in New York City's Manhattan. Also, the people here exercise extremely enthusiastically. I have never seen a place where people work so hard to be fit. I asked, "Is fitness and fashion the purpose of living here?" My friend answered, "Yes, that's the purpose." The most notable thing was that I spent the whole day at the beach with many people, but I didn't see anyone smoking. The beach is clean, and there is almost no trash anywhere.

I then flew back to New York City and visited more clients in the surrounding areas. After years of doing business with American companies, I can only say they are very practical, fast and cool. Their business culture is completely different from Vietnamese culture. But, the US is a large and not too fastidious market, suitable for the development of Vietnamese businesses. They are still one of the best options!

And other things ...

On my last day in the US, I visited a customer in Philadelphia. I went with a close friend named Kai, an Asian merchandise dealer. We talked the whole way. He came to America with his family because his father had worked for the United Nations decades ago. He is the only Asian in the five largest agency offices in the US.

I asked the white owner of the all-white employee office, "If there are any qualified Asians for an interview, will you accept it?"

He said, "Yes."

"So why have I worked with the US market for over 15 years, but only one Asian is an agent in the field of Commodities and Spices?" This guy laughed.

That made me think of a story I have kept to myself for a long time. Vietnam supplies 30 percent of the world's coffee production. Accordingly, many companies worldwide are opening representative offices with many foreign employees. These foreign employees have far more benefits compared to Vietnamese employees. A brand-new intern, a study-abroad student, can do research or go abroad to visit. They can meet apprentices and do business. While Vietnamese employees, after many years of dedicated work, rarely go abroad outside of business meetings. I dare not ask my friends why foreigners hold the Chief Representative position of the office. Or, like British and American actors, who only acted in one or two famous movies receive such high salaries from a film, when actors from other countries, including the European Union (except the UK), don't experience such benefits. Alas, I have my own answer for that.

At Phuc Sinh system, we send Vietnamese employees everywhere, to Asia, Europe and America. Dozens of people have the opportunity to interact with partners, work, cross paths and develop. In 2016, we reaped the benefits of the previous four to five years of continuous investment in employees by using a fair structure.

Relating back to meeting customers, agents and partners: I find Kai smart, very good and sensitive, with a decent selling point. I've known him for a long time, maybe 15 years. In the early years of knowing him, Kai was young and fit. Unfortunately, after his divorce, his life had come very hard. In New York, life seems hard for everyone who belongs to the middle-class and below. The cost of living was expensive, and the work was stressful. The realities were far from those of Ho Chi Minh City, although the comparison is inequitable. Companies around the world have their ups and downs. In the early years, we did a lot of business together, contracts around the clock. After that, Kai's personal life was affected, so his business performance decreased significantly. While on board, we discussed how to get business back on track. I lightly blame them for being lackadaisical in sustaining the business market. Any American company will, at some point, face obstacles. Building a company is challenging. Keeping it is even harder, especially if the contracts are lost to competitors.

After the conversation, the agent where Kai worked seemed to really want a change. The next morning, Kai's boss came to my hotel for breakfast and talked very cordially.

That's business: If you show your partner your business is really good and has many options, the partner will treat you much better. If you simply have them as a partner … they won't immediately, but will gradually become less interested in you. Of course, if you don't provide many services and only have one partner, that's your choice.

One thing I learned about many customers by visiting these countries is that, after appraising Phuc Sinh's quality and services, they want to be the only buyers in their market. Moreover, I tried to make it so every good buyer could buy our products. We always strive for quality and service, and they must always try to be good customers in terms of prestige, volume and payment. Such is life.

Thinking about Asians and Vietnamese working in the US reminds me more of education in Vietnam. Many families now invest a lot of money and time in their children. The father and mother will take turns in taking them to school. The family pays a lot for the child to go to school, and they study very well. Investing in children is a very natural series of sacrifices from parents to grandparents. However, Vietnam is not always the country that sees the return on that investment. If there is a good student, overseas funds may come to seek them out. They will invite them to participate in competitions, select the best students, give them scholarships to train abroad and provide attractive incentives. So, after much investment, we've lost a person who has gone to work for companies abroad. Of course, everyone needs personal development, and everyone has the right to choose what is best for his or her growth. Although the family invests a lot in their children, companies and governments can choose the most quintessential and best graduate. Since it's a business, I also know that if they hire good employees, they can bring in profits ten times more than their salary.

I was a fan of the TV Show Road to Olympia. When I read the newspaper, I saw that almost 100 percent of the winners live in Australia and work as teachers or lecturers at Australian universities. However, the values they bring and what they contribute to Vietnam and society are less! I wondered: Why has such a famous competition show become just a university lecturer contest for Australian schools? Why … so cheap? This is not something I can answer.

I used to believe high-quality products with attractive packaging and affordable prices would guarantee domestic distribution success. However, I now realize this may have been naive thinking. It's possible that even if I have all these qualities, I could still be rejected simply because I'm not part of the "gang." Why do distributors not "take" clean goods, or why do users still prefer coffee mixed with corn, flavorings, chemicals, and other mysterious ingredients? Maybe more time and patience are needed. Success and failure are always intertwined for me. But failure to see how we need to try, and failure itself, are good factors for each person. It allows us to keep our feet on the ground, close to reality. And to especially feel that we are not too good for the field in which we failed!

I also need to adapt more to the "Vietnam reality" in an effort to not stray away from the business principle: "quality is a commitment" of the company itself ...

The first few lines of the year, the story of West to East, starting with the latest trip, are all experiences for me. That's life! Studying, persevering in trying and gaining knowledge is still a daily task for each of us ...

Ho Chi Minh City, 2016.

PRICE OF ART

It's been a year now that I have no longer bought paintings. I merely look upon them in galleries, or at the ones in my own collection. With the development of the art market, many things have changed too quickly and, along the way, have led to some unfortunate changes.

The last five years have seen considerable economic development, as well as an increased general income. The middle-class has more money. Though they expressed little interest in the arts before, they do now. They now spend more money on paintings, which has pushed the general price to a new level.

Five or six years ago, there were plenty of beautiful paintings at rather affordable prices. That is no longer the case. Now painters want to sell their paintings at much higher prices. They even compete with each other to see who can sell their artworks at the greatest price, rather than focusing on the beauty of the art. The price at which their art is sold determines their artistry level, not the piece's beauty. We have plenty of painters, and 5,000 art students graduate from universities every year. Yet, truly brilliant artists are quite difficult to find. People would talk about Mai Trung Thu, Le Pho ... and further, Tran Luu Hau, Dang Xuan Hoa, Nguyen Trung and Ho Huu Thu. When the GDP growth rate achieved 7 percent per year, Vietnamese people started to pay more attention to paintings and spend more money. Eventually, there will be no great paintings left.

While it was easy finding Nguyen Trung's or Tran Luu Hau's paintings five or six years ago, now they cannot be found even in famous galleries. Vietnamese collectors seem to have swept them all clean. Nguyen Trung's paintings have disappeared from all galleries. Tran Luu Hau's are very limited and no longer of the same caliber as the ones before.

There are still artists whose paintings have kept their beauty, like Ho Huu Thu, Pham Luan, Dang Xuan Hoa and Dao Hai Phong, though the number of such talented artists is few. Thus, when people buy more, there will inevitably be very few great paintings left. That's also why galleries no longer have pieces that urge you to buy them. When you start collecting paintings, you always strive to find ones that give off an irresistible feeling that you have to buy them. But now, even that is becoming rare.

Moreover, when society developed, it was quite normal to pay US$300 to US$500 for a painting in the past. But when housing prices go up, and the cost of living also goes up during such development, artists also wish to sell their paintings at very high prices. When the demand for beautiful paintings increased, artists sought to paint more, increasing the price of paintings. This can hold some truth, but focusing too heavily on the price of a painting while creating it often results in a mediocre painting. Experienced buyers can surely recognize that.

True collectors will probably only spend a lot of money when they feel the artist has truly dedicated themselves to the painting unconditionally, offering everything to it. The painting will exude a beauty that the collector cannot resist. I still remember, five or six years ago, when I went to buy paintings. I must say that there were many beautiful paintings on the market at that time, and few people bought them. The paintings of Nguyen Trung, Tran Luu Hau and Dang Xuan Hoa were truly wonderful. Now there are very few paintings available by them. Almost none exist. Some artists are now so "creative" that their paintings have less sparkle, which makes me nostalgic for the old days.

However, it must also be recognized that Vietnamese people collect many paintings as the economy develops. This pushes the prices of paintings much higher than four or five years ago. The fine arts have a different place in the spiritual lives of many individuals and families. To a certain extent, the increased price level shows that domestic and international collectors appreciate the value of Vietnamese fine art more. However, the devaluation factor of the currency must be excluded.

Regarding Tran Luu Hau: I have had the opportunity to see many of his paintings in catalogs, in his books or in the gallery releases. His paintings are beautiful, but foreigners buy most of them, even hundreds of them. The best paintings they bought were from the late 80s to the early 90s. If they saw a good painting, they would buy it. The price was very cheap at that time. In the early 2000s, his paintings began to receive more attention. They were collected and bought by Vietnamese people. The price of his paintings increased. From 2010 to 2015, many Vietnamese people collected his paintings, and prices reached a new level. Recently, I saw that Tran Luu Hau's paintings were priced three and four times higher than five years ago. An average-sized Flower painting, 60x80cm, was almost US$60,000. The 110x135cm Boat was already US$100,000, an incredibly large leap.

It is the same with Dang Xuan Hoa: His paintings have increased in price by 50 percent in just the last two years. Demand for his paintings has increased strongly, and his paintings in the gallery are now offered at very high prices. It's funny that most buyers of Dang Xuan Hoa's paintings are not Singaporeans anymore, but mainly Vietnamese.

Nguyen Trung's paintings also increased greatly in price. Before, it was easy to find a painting by Nguyen Trung in Saigon galleries; now, there are almost none. A 100x100cm painting of his can be bought for between US$50,000 and US$60,000. Although at auction companies, his paintings are much more expensive.

Ho Huu Thu's, Pham Luan's, and Dao Hai Phong's paintings have also increased in price continuously. Ho Huu Thu's work has a ghostly beauty. His paintings have recently been sought after by collectors. Paintings are reaching up to US$45,000 or even US$60,000 for larger-sized pieces.

Looking at this, I am very pleased with the Vietnamese art market. There has been a big change in art collections and prices over the last five years. The number of Vietnamese people involved in the art trade and buying expensive paintings has greatly increased. However, we do not have an independent trade center to auction large paintings in Vietnam. Additionally, there are no painting appraisal centers.

It is undeniable that Vietnamese paintings are beautiful; however, markets in Singapore or Hong Kong are still far ahead. Vietnam is still far behind neighboring markets, like the Philippines and Indonesia. They have a team of locals who buy many paintings from local artists. For example, Indonesian businessmen spend a lot of money to buy paintings and promote the art market there.

This is the situation of the domestic Vietnamese painting market. While overseas, the market is very prosperous; we are witnessing a series of new records for the prices of Vietnamese paintings. In the past, we only saw paintings of foreign artists reaching millions of US dollars, such as in China, Indonesia, and other countries in the East. It has only been in the last three or four years we have heard about Vietnamese paintings earning millions of dollars. The leading artist who received the most attention was Le Pho. What's even better is that in the past, only foreigners who bought for their personal collections paid the highest prices for Vietnamese paintings. Yet, we have heard of Vietnamese people buying paintings at Hong Kong auction rooms and paying the highest prices for Vietnamese paintings. Vietnamese paintings have amounted to millions of dollars. It has been a huge change from home to abroad.

In fact, if you want an artist's paintings to be expensive, you must first buy them and make them valuable. Only when many buyers of Vietnamese paintings respect, appreciate and pay high prices for Vietnamese Artists' work shall Vietnamese paintings enter the ranks of expensive paintings worldwide.

BUSINESS CULTURE

In 2018, many Free Trade Agreements (FTAs) came to life. Some agreements had been approved by countries/blocks with Vietnam. Along with that, we also witnessed a huge wave of foreign investment in Vietnam. In the agricultural sector, when a Free Trade Agreement showed signs of mutual understanding between the European Union and Vietnam, we saw a lot of European companies investing in this industry. They opened warehouses and manufactured and built factories. Many European companies have only opened offices in Vietnam in the last 20 years, but when there were signs of the agreement being approved, they immediately invested more. A company with a warehouse or factory could expand and increase production, leading to fierce competition at all levels. Companies will find it harder to recruit and will have to pay more attractive salaries and benefits to incentivize employees to join their company. In terms of production and business activity, companies will have to compete fiercely for both production and sales of raw materials. Businesses will become increasingly competitive.

When we saw Singapore and Hong Kong businesses competing with European businesses a decade ago, we wondered why we couldn't be like them. We found ways to sell to European and American buyers with less involvement of intermediaries so that we could sell more. When Europeans and Americans came to Vietnam to open warehouses and factories, we thought not only must we compete with them in the Vietnamese market ... but we must improve our services and compete with them in Europe and America, forcing them to make efforts to survive.

We have been recruiting sales representatives in central European countries and the US, bringing goods to their countries to sell, and transshipping to improve services. We sought to sell bulk goods at bonded warehouses in Europe and the US.

We also went to Brazil and Indonesia to buy peppercorn and coffee to sell to Middle Eastern, European, and American buyers. When customers buy coffee and peppercorn, we sell products originating from Vietnam, Brazil, Indonesia and India, among others. We seek to provide customers with a variety of services, with the feeling that everything is available. We can only compete with buyers in the tough Vietnam market by approaching the buyer's markets.

We continuously develop new products because I think expanding profit is impossible while relying solely on old products.

The old cannot compete with the new from other companies, so we continuously make new products whenever opportunities and conditions exist. The Phuc Sinh Son La project is a challenging and captivating project. Son La has grown coffee for over 35 years. Their coffee is excellent, but few people know about it, and almost no one has invested in building a complete factory. Thirty-five years is a very long time. In the North, many businesses pour money into the South, investing in coffee. Yet, they have not invested in building a factory in Son La. There are companies that buy coffee from the people or produce it themselves. However, due to asynchronous investment, the coffee made is not delicious or unique and cannot be sold at a good price. There have been many instances when prices increased, and the coffee was transported to the Central Highlands of Lam Dong, Da Lat and mixed with Arabica and Robusta coffee to sell. If Son La Arabica coffee is not delicious, it would be one thing, yet over here Son La coffee has been very good for so many years. What a pity!

The first time we came to Son La was in March 2017. We immediately felt that Son La had wonderful land for growing coffee. Accordingly, we built a factory. We had the support of our colleagues and the authorities. After eight months of construction, we had a factory with machinery imported from Colombia. We invited customers and big companies worldwide to Son La, allowing them to see the newly built factory, the imported equipment, and the complete wastewater treatment system. A survey of the actual planting areas in Son La revealed an A quality grade. Soon after, we exported coffee under the brand name K Coffee Blue Son La, and it was well-received by our customers.

It has been incredibly effective and beneficial. We have good and delicious products for our export business, people don't have to transport goods to the Central Highlands to sell, and the company has created many jobs for the local people of Son La. Nothing can compare! As Blue Son La coffee travels worldwide, we are very happy because we are both doing business and contributing to a better life in the region.

When I entered the business, I saw a lot of challenges that I needed to overcome. Traveling from Ho Chi Minh City to Europe takes 13 hours. Going from Saigon to Son La takes 11 hours – almost a day, during the daytime, while one can travel to Europe by night, sleep, and the next morning can work.

Moreover, transporting 20' FCL containers from Hai Phong or Saigon to a major European port costs US$700. Towing containers from Son La to Hai Phong costs 15 million VND (more than US$650), and from Son La to Saigon costs 30 million VND! Almost as a joke, the cost in Vietnam is unbelievably high.

I often go on business trips to different regions in Vietnam, and we have toll stations. Coming to Binh Duong, automatic toll collection is very easy. When returning to Saigon, though, the toll collection is very different. There is almost no automatic method, requiring you to stick your neck out of the car to pay. Going down to Dong Nai is the same. Changing to automatic toll collection in the southern provinces or across the country wouldn't be difficult. All it takes is the governing body or leader to set a deadline for automating toll booths; then we can go all over Vietnam without having to stick our neck out to pay. It simply requires one to buy a prepaid scanner. This would reduce many traffic jams to the airport or anywhere, saving time and lots of money.

The new year is coming. Like every year, we try to work hard creatively. We constantly hope for a peaceful world with more changes for the better.

WHY DOESN'T VIETNAMESE COFFEE HAVE A GLOBAL BRAND YET?

Vietnam stands second in coffee exportation, with nearly 30 million bags, or 1.8 million tons annually. Almost all countries, from developing to developed, buy coffee from Vietnam. In Spain, 70 percent of the coffee consumed in their country is from Vietnam. But why, when it comes to Vietnamese coffee, do very few know about it? Italy uses almost the same amount of coffee, and some of Italy's most famous brands use up to 70 percent of Vietnamese coffee, Germany too. But when asked about coffee, many mention Colombia, India, and even Indonesia, but not Vietnam. We export 30 million bags, Colombia 14 million bags, and Indonesia 10 million bags. Why is our coffee in such a state?

We have been producing strongly for the past 30 years. Our customers say that 25 years ago we only shipped four to five million bags. Due to the rapid growth, we only sell coffee at low quality. An opinion has circulated until now that we only care about selling in volume and having foreign currency revenue, that we almost forget about quality jobs on a larger scale.

Asking large coffee export enterprises, they just want to sell more. Large coffee export enterprises just want to sell more – and quickly. Since there is almost no immediate profit, they forget about quality. They invest very little in the quality and promotion of Vietnamese coffee. Moreover, the apathy is quite high, with interest only in selling around Saigon, not promoting and introducing it to the world.

Promoting trade for us is like viewing flowers, mainly just to travel and shop. We planned well, but the staff was distracted, with little to no concern for the business. This is so normal and familiar that no one felt bothered.

We were sponsored to go to the fair at trade markets, but so many stalls lacked staff. They were either engrossed in going out or leaving early, leaving the booths empty.

Let's look at booths like those of Indonesia and India: They sent a team of experts to introduce the tasting quality and did a great job promoting said quality. There were dozens of people, inside and outside, with international guests attending. That is how Indonesia, India, and Colombia, not to mention countries like Brazil, represent themselves well, from farmers to businesses. Since India and Indonesia care a lot about quality, their customers also feel it and expect high quality from those countries, so they pay high prices. It is mainly because businesses in these countries do very well in marketing.

We often complain that we don't have the money to promote like Indonesia, an agricultural exporter much less than us. But the truth is that Indonesia sends all the experts who know the quality of their coffee to introduce it to international customers. While we only send marketing people to offices, and employees to travel and shop.

Vietnamese Arabica coffee has been on the market for over 30 years, but many do not know this. Over ten years ago, we produced a large amount of Arabica, and the world's buyers were excited about Vietnam. But as it happens, the quality was not stable. One container could have up to ten different types of quality, with others having high quality and the remainder being very different or poor. Buyers were then very cautious and had very low confidence in our coffee.

All these factors led to our Arabica products selling for US$2,200 per ton FOB[11] this season, while Indonesia's quality Arabica products can sell for US$6,000 to US$8,000 per ton; that's sad.

I do business in coffee, so sometimes going out in the world makes me feel sad. People in this country drink corn coffee and

---

11 FOB is an abbreviation in English for the word Free on board, which means that the delivery of goods waives the responsibility of the seller when the goods have been loaded on board the ship. That is, when the goods have not been on the ship, all responsibility will be on the seller, and after the goods have been on the ship, all responsibility will be on the buyer.

chemical soybean coffee. As for our exports, the price is not high, and we are almost caught in a situation where we can barely make a profit. The more I try, and the more I go, the more I realize we have to find another, more sustainable way for the industry.

In 2015, we started to make specialty coffee for Robusta BLUE OCEAN (Specialty Robusta). Looking at India making Robusta coffee, I think I have to be determined. The factory was completed at the end of 2015, and we produced and introduced our coffee to customers. I remember when I went to the luxury goods fair to present, a French customer was surprised when I said that Vietnam has a specialty coffee shop. We indeed have special coffee production, though very small: by individuals or just a few shops, not large quantities. I persist in making quality coffee to introduce to international guests.

In 2016 and 2017, we continuously introduced and sent tasting samples to our guests. It was great that by the 2018 Holland Fair at the start of the year, we had been accepted by our customers. Many coffee buyers have ordered our Robusta BLUE OCEAN, especially customers who always demand high-quality coffee from Switzerland, Germany and Italy. This was unprecedented and a great thing, a "certification" of prestigious, high-quality goods from Vietnam.

Son La, why did I come?

My friend and I went to visit the Northwest and went to Son La. I was very surprised at the lush land there, which is very similar to the Central Highlands. Son La also grows a lot of coffee.

I had heard of Son La, albeit with very little information. I was surprised about the area and output the day we arrived. I took Son La Arabica coffee, roasted, ground, and tried it. It was delicious and flavorful, far different from Central Highlands Arabica coffee. Perhaps it is the sun and wind here, the four seasons with spring, summer, autumn and winter. The altitude and soil are good, so they have created products with very different and complex flavors. The intention to build a high-class processing factory began. I carefully surveyed and sent project and quality staff to survey. The results were quite positive.

The more I investigated, the more I realized there was much unrealized potential for the coffee here. Over 30 years of cultivation without a name, though the quality was excellent. Traders just bought it to mix with Da Lat and Lam Dong coffee, even with Robusta. Traders did this so much that the province itself also believed the same about the worth of their crop. They set a very low price, lower than Da Lat coffee. This was probably partly because Son La had no high-end and complete processing plant. Or, production was too fragmented, and there was a lack of confidence and understanding. Not a single batch of containers or large shipments had been exported under the name of Son La Arabica coffee. The more I surveyed, the more opportunities I saw for myself, Phuc Sinh, and Son La coffee. We applied for a factory building permit and received enthusiastic support from the province. After eight months of construction, Phuc Sinh's employees, managers, and partners completed it with much fine effort.

On the opening day, we invited many domestic and foreign partners from all over the world to Ho Chi Minh City, and from there flew to Hanoi, then to Son La to attend the event at the factory and taste the coffee. BLUE OCEAN for Robusta specialty coffee and BLUE SON LA for washed Arabica. It must be said that it was amazing. Customers praised and appreciated our level of quality. There were many orders for BLUE SON LA and BLUE OCEAN. I strongly believe that the quality of Vietnamese coffee will reach far and that all coffee-drinking people of Vietnam will recognize the quality of Vietnamese coffee.

It was a pleasure to contribute to building a brand for myself, as well as the Vietnamese coffee industry, and a brand for Vietnam. This is never easy; it takes self-trust to find good coffee and figure out how to process it, especially how to introduce it to commercial importers and consumers worldwide.

HAPPY THOUGHTS DURING COVID

One day I sat for lunch at the office restaurant. Next to my friend was the Human Resources Director. She told a story so enthralling that, even though I was sitting at the next table, I had to pay attention and listen. She was telling it so clearly, and in the end, I came with my bowl to join her table and listen to the story.

Covid-19: A Harsh Test

She said her children attended a private school. On the first day, instead of 300 students attending, there were only about 50. We asked why and learned that many parents had returned to their hometowns or moved elsewhere. "Covid-19 made everything too harsh, and when I realized that the company was still paying the full salary, I felt extremely lucky. My children still went to school and were not too disturbed. Naturally, I fell in love with the company and the director," she said. After lunch, I went back to work with a feeling of gratitude/happiness.

A niece-in-law came over to my house to eat and talk. I asked her where she worked. Out of six Korean factories for leather shoes, only two factories had work at that time. She worked at one of the two factories twice a week; the salary being for two working days per week. Yet, many employees were laid off at the end of their contracts because there was so little work. She said, "Fortunately, my husband still works full time and has enough of a salary; otherwise, it would be difficult. Uncle, I feel very lucky and happy."

Often, when we want young people to experience and appreciate the present, we let them go on charity trips to disadvantaged rural areas. They see and experience things they never had before and meet hard-working people. Those encounters can allow young people to appreciate their parents and family more because they understand that they're very lucky when comparing what they have seen with their circumstances.

Sometimes we are unhappy and feel inadequate all the time. Unhappiness arises because we keep struggling with work and other factors within ourselves. Like a child whose parents are too protective, and the child finds everything normal; that is until, at some point in their life, they encounter big problems and have many regrets, then life really gets hard.

I still remember when I set up a trading company at the age of 25. A few years later, our business was grossing hundreds of millions of dollars, which equated to thousands of billions of dongs. People asked where the money came from to do business. They knew me from when I migrated to the South; I had no money at first. I told them I had a client from France; He was the fifth generation of his family in that business, and he was doing business with me. They then heard the story of what led me to Natexis Bank of France, and I convinced them to give me a loan. Then there were customers from America, Italy, and Ireland, doing business with me. They heard my business story, how I earnt hundreds of thousands of dollars by faxing invoices. Customers from Singapore led me to Singapore UOB Bank to guarantee some more loans. I told that to anyone who asked, and they didn't believe it. No one believed fairy tales could happen in real life! They said I couldn't tell convincing stories or play poker. I just laughed, but felt very lucky!

Sharing is also happiness!

Being positive, believing in life, and working hard to make a happy living is an enormous challenge for many people. To live a happy life, you must create a happy environment, a joyful environment. You must live without hiding your heart. Sharing money is also creating a happy environment.

As I was born amid difficult times, when I saw people going places, and going abroad, I wanted this for myself, my managers and my employees to have an abundance of such opportunities. I do not hesitate to invest my money by investing in human resources. That also makes me happy, living unselfishly, even if only I know about it.

So what is the role of a leader? It is to bring about the best development for the employees.

We also invested in the office building without hesitating to spend money on the proper facilities and working conditions for our employees. When I see the employees are happy and excited, I also feel happy.

Covid-19 has brought many things to a halt. But in a way, the world has seen benefits: the sea is cleaner, some fish populations have been restored, the forests have experienced regrowth, and the air is clearer. The question is: Can we stop for a moment to feel the happiness in each of our own lives?

Covid-19 happened. Due to the loss during this pandemic, we had to sit back. While sitting in that state of retreat, looking back, I found everything I had was more beautiful. I felt so lucky and happy! Fortunately, I still have a job now and can fully pay my staff of several hundred people. Sometimes happiness means looking back with gratitude. To look back at the enthusiastic dedication to work and to see overflowing love for the work by my staff.

Covid-19 made everything difficult, but it did not stop us. At least we could share and overcome difficulties together. For me, that is luck and happiness. How do you feel?

A PUNGENT YEAR – A BITTER-SWEET YEAR

When closing a year of many scenarios, businessmen will sit back and reflect to capture the promising signs of green crops for the next year.

From business-to-business (B2B), then continuing to expand business-to-consumer (B2C), I didn't feel the difficulty and difference when I first started. It was also the beginning of what turned out to be the arduous journey of the past year, Ky Hoi.

International Coffee Business – Harsh 2019!

The coffee industry in 2019 was full of tension and fluctuation. Coffee prices in London and New York fell to their lowest level in 15 years, pushing growers and businesses toward difficulty. They struggled to survive. The difficulty was even worse for traders around the world, as well as for coffee exporters and small collectors. This was all due to many objective and subjective influences that created a domino effect.

According to normal business rules, when the price of coffee on the London floor goes down, the price of coffee from producing and supplying countries will also decrease. Surprisingly, in the case of 2019, the price of coffee from the producing countries went up because farmers there had recently chosen not to sell at low prices.

Vietnamese coffee farmers who used to store coffee in warehouses or sell to collecting traders now keep it at their homes. In the past, when farmers stored their coffee in warehouses, they'd be left with no stock when the price went up. They would lose a lot of money. Because of such incidents, the general farmer has now decided to only sell at their set price. In other words, they were claiming the right to determine the market.

All traders of agricultural products do pre-sale, so they have to buy goods for delivery according to contracts. This forces coffee to become scarce at the source of purchase, despite the price on the exchange floor, which causes the entire coffee export business worldwide to face the problem of buying high and selling low. Many traders have had to give up the game.

After 18 years of doing business globally in the agricultural industry, it can be said that I have never had to take the reins in running an arduous business like the Ky Hoi year. If someone asks me which year is the most difficult for business, I will say each year has difficulty.

Domestic Coffee Business: Starting again after three years!

In Vietnam, doing coffee business directly with consumers has taught Phuc Sinh extremely valuable lessons. Our company costs in the past period equal the entire three years of starting up in the FMCG (fast-moving consumer goods) industry.

Along with the cost of time, we must pay the price for trust in choosing and using human resources. Phuc Sinh started the domestic coffee business with our "K Coffee" roasted and ground coffee brand in 2015. We entered the market as a top ten exporter of Vietnamese coffee, owning a factory right in the coffee growing areas of Dak Lak, Buon Ma Thuot with UTZ, BRC, and Halal standard farms. Phuc Sinh's agricultural products, since meeting the above standards, have been recognized by retailers, food service companies and manufacturers worldwide.

With clear methods and a firm foundation from the very beginning, in the stages of raw materials and production, our message of quality and hard work is conveyed by providing the market with High-quality, 100 percent pure coffee products. This ensures healthy, safe and delicious drinks for all Vietnamese consumers. K Coffee launched with the first lines of roasted ground and instant coffee. When marketed to consumers accordingly, it had been supported by many partners and customers. To develop the system and product lines by brand, I outsourced the consulting and hired a CEO to run the work at a specialized FMCG company (Phuc Sinh Consumer).

Determining that I had no experience in the home market, I chose to hire a CEO who was a marketing person having experience in many large domestic FMCG enterprises. I did not manage directly at the subsidiary but assigned it to the CEO. As a result, I've had many CEO-Marketers in three years. During the tenure of each manager, they all shared quite similar characteristics. They all made a series of huge plans – including spending money – until they left behind a pile of accounting books with many serious imbalances. Furthermore, KPI targets were never met. The parent company then had to step in, clean up, and continue to invest anew.

By the end of 2018, Phuc Sinh Consumer had experienced a third restructuring phase. An employee had quit, and a partner of Phuc Sinh introduced his friend to the position of CEO in a subsidiary. Normally at Phuc Sinh, we cooperate in recruiting with the most famous employers in Vietnam. However, experience at the FMCG company had shown us it was necessary to expand the recruitment channel more broadly, yet selectively, in finding a manager that met expectations. Because I was in charge of sales at Phuc Sinh company, the efficiency was still very high among many things. However, I didn't feel ready to run the consumer goods segment myself. Therefore, I agreed to continue recruiting new CEOs for FMCG worldwide and considered recommendations from friends; I also accepted the huge salary that went with hiring the CEOs.

As usual, when taking over the management position, the new CEO of Phuc Sinh Consumer also made a huge revenue commitment. But after nearly a year, the actual revenue only achieved 20 percent of the plan. All the while, the retailers continuously pushed back expired and returned goods because they were not satisfied with the service and inventory. Moreover, the accounting system reported a series of debts with suppliers, agents, distributors, and other associates of the subsidiary. I was willing to work with the new CEO; I asked for an explanation for these serious issues in order to resolve the backlog. This person immediately submitted a resignation letter and demanded to be paid the salary according to the negotiated terms for terminating the contract. We proposed to pay only the salary in the last month and temporarily postpone the late payment for half a month to review all debts incurred during this person's time in charge of the company. We also had to re-evaluate all agreement contents according to the labor contract. This employee's reaction was to sue me via the District Trade Union Office. If that wasn't enough, he provided inaccurate information about Phuc Sinh to a few media outlets with which he had a relationship. They wrote public articles, pressured me, distorted the company's image, and caused a real headache.

Looking back on the old story, Phuc Sinh had a year of losing money and an inefficient investment period for the goal of expanding FMCG. The B2C industry is really difficult. If you just do B2B successfully, you can immediately invade B2C as desired. Above all, the greater pain for me was feeling like I had been tricked, in a subtle and planned manner, by a manager I had delegated authority to and trusted.

However, I still think my biggest mistake was because I was weak in recruiting and trusted the wrong person! Of course, after realizing I was wrong, I immediately corrected it. I decided I would be the one to rebuild from scratch – directly in charge of the management and operation of the Phuc Sinh Consumer system – determined to continue to fulfill the goal of bringing the best-quality consumer products to Vietnam so that Vietnamese people could enjoy delicious, clean agricultural products originating from their own country!

A Bright Signal for 2020

In a confused mood, I met a friend from the same industry. This person predicted I might lose a lot, but I still had something to gain: K Coffee is delicious and of good quality, so consumers will still support it. Only when losing consumers is everything lost! Changing management means changing how the company operates for better service and customer care, so consumers will continue to have the confidence to come to Phuc.

I embarked on the task of handling old debts and developing Phuc Sinh Consumer into the right "rail" of an FMCG company. I expanded distribution systems, customer care services, supermarkets, purchasing partners, etc. For Phuc Sinh Consumer, customers are the focus – They are most important. We gradually changed our services and the way we reached consumers.

As a result, after a few months of these changes, K Coffee's sales improved. I was able to pay off all supplier, dealer and distributor debts. The outstanding problems at the subsidiary left by the old management were eliminated. The orders were steady and growing larger and larger. Phuc Sinh's factories ran two shifts per day of continuous production to prepare for the Tet season.

Another breakthrough came at the end of 2019 when we introduced the freeze-dried peppercorn product to the Vietnamese market. This was this product's debut in Vietnam, but Phuc Sinh had been distributing it worldwide for nearly a year.

Along with freeze-dried peppercorn, we also launched green peppercorn, black peppercorn and white peppercorn sauce and sold them on our online purchasing page "www.kphucsinh.vn." This particular line of peppercorn sauce has been exported for five years. Until now, we are the only company in Vietnam that has exported this product. Everyone was very supportive and welcoming of the new products. I think the hardest things are no longer the past year's challenges but the difficulties that would have existed if we hadn't made a really great product.

Closing a year of many scenarios, I want to remember the promising signs for green crops in the coming year. It was the launch of freeze-dried green peppercorn, an online sales website trusted by customers "kphucsinh.vn." Many factories of Phuc Sinh in Binh Duong, Son La, and Dak Lak had been expanded and completed, the management of member companies had stabilized, and plenty of other hopeful things. The rush of orders promised a prosperous New Year not only for Phuc Sinh but also attested to the purchasing power – the big attractive selling force ahead of the market.

An intense year has left a warm taste, like K Peppercorn is the true spice of business and life, making me and my colleagues believe as we did before. We shall continue to put trust in people and projects in the Year of the Rat ...

End of the Year of the Pig, 2019.

365 DAYS OF CONNECTION

There were many tough challenges in 2019. A lot of negative information makes us forget about the many achievements and the good news.

Telecommunications Services Connecting the World

Because of the nature of my work, I often travel abroad. Connecting to telecommunications systems can be problematic when we go to another country. If we don't turn off roaming, sometimes a day or two of international roaming amounts to several tens of millions of dongs in bills when we return home.

Many experienced people choose to buy a SIM card abroad or, more recently, a portable Wi-Fi transmitter. Even so, it is still extremely inconvenient having to carry two phones. The vast majority choose to rarely connect with customers and company colleagues when on business trips, only doing so when returning to their hotels.

Meanwhile, I have a lot of clients who come to Vietnam and still use their home country's cell phone numbers while here. I asked them: how is this possible with such expensive roaming fees? They say they have a contract with the telecommunications service provider in their country.

I secretly wish that Vietnam would also have such multinational agreements to provide Vietnamese businesses, entrepreneurs, international students and people generally with such convenience when traveling the globe.

However, in the last few years, mobile companies and telecommunications services have improved their services. Receiving a text message in a foreign country no longer requires one to run to buy a Sim card or carry a Wi-Fi adapter. Things are constantly changing, as with internet platforms. Every corner of our business and life is moving and changing at a tremendous speed.

You only need to spend 200,000–300,000 VND to connect to the host country's telecommunications services network and freely receive messages through Viber, WhatsApp, Skype, etc.

Connecting with colleagues and customers is now very easy everywhere you go. This is extremely stimulating for the development and maintenance of business connections. For a person who travels abroad like me, it helps to stay connected and keep on top of the situation.

Furthermore, it's amazing that the US telecom and 4G charges are the cheapest. It's almost as cheap as paying for a telecom company in Vietnam. Recently, I traveled with a delegation from the Ministry of Agriculture and Rural Development and sharing this service made everyone very excited to hear that it was so cheap and the utility extremely convenient.

It can be said that with just a telecommunications connection, the flat world is now even flatter!

Aviation Takes Wings to Fly Across the Sky

Due to the nature of my work, I am constantly traveling by plane. I secretly wished for a long time that Vietnam's airlines had direct flights to the places where I work. Transiting is very arduous and time-consuming. Fortunately, my wishes have come true many times in the past few years.

I really enjoy going to Europe for business. Since it is a straight flight, I just take a long sleep and arrive where I need to be. It's great! In just five years, we have accomplished a lot.

However, I still wish I could get a direct flight from Ho Chi Minh City to New York. Airlines don't consider the large populations of Ho Chi Minh or Hanoi when they draw up their flight schedules. Why can Singapore, Thailand, and Hong Kong make it and become big transit hubs, but we can't?

Vietnam has the advantage of burgeoning tourism, and many people are quite familiar with our service. We just need to be more confident! I still remember pondering the question of why Germany, Hong Kong, Singapore, and the Netherlands could conduct cross-border trade around the world; why couldn't Vietnam? Thanks to such inquiries, we have implemented border transfer for decades now: buying from Indonesia and Brazil, selling to Europe and the US, and creating many more opportunities.

One more wish of mine is that Son La had an airport. Phuc Sinh has a factory in Son La, and our route is intricate every time we travel there from Ho Chi Minh City. First, we must fly to Hanoi and then travel the rest of the way by road. It takes a whole day to get there, which is nearly as long as going from Ho Chi Minh City to Frankfurt. But to Frankfurt, we can comfortably fly through the night.

The southern region would have easy access to resources if an air route existed. Plus, the people here would have the opportunity to travel and invest in the Northwest, contributing to the development of this remote region which has great untapped potential for strong development.

The Internet moves all fields into motion like a hurricane

At Phuc Sinh, when we sell coffee and peppercorn consumables under the brands K Coffee and K Peppercorn, customers always ask where they can buy them. This is difficult and inconvenient if the product is not widely available for distribution systems. Therefore, we built an online eCommerce site at www.kphucsinh.vn.

We tested it for a year, and on November 26, 2019, the site went live as we simultaneously launched freeze-dried green peppercorn and peppercorn sauce for the first time in Vietnam and worldwide. I couldn't imagine thousands of orders being placed on the online sales page right after the launch at kphucsinh.vn.

Everyone responded that ordering on the site was easy and fast. We were delighted that people from all parts of the country could place orders, and we could deliver delicious pure coffee and peppercorn everywhere.

Epilogue

During the past five years, I have often felt that there have been many areas of significant progress for us. I hope my wishes will come true in the coming years, and I will be able to fly directly to the US and Son La from Ho Chi Minh City with Vietnam Airlines. Then we will reach further and faster through every step of the journey ahead!

2019

END-OF-YEAR REFLECTION 3

Sitting down at the end of the year, as usual, I want to write about the past year. Everything seems to have stopped. This year I couldn't see a lot of joy, perhaps due to the many challenges and difficulties in 2020. As we approach the end of the year, there is little sign of the bustle with Christmas and New Year's songs we usually see from mid-November onward every year on the city streets. As someone who writes regularly, I always think to myself: "Just sit down and try to write. As usual, there is a lot of information, but it is not always easy to start."

At the end of 2019, when I heard the news of the developing epidemic in Wuhan, I felt that something terrible was about to happen. I knew overcoming it would be difficult, so I met with the company's staff. I shared my feeling that the world would soon be in an extremely difficult situation, and we would have to find ways to overcome it. I stressed we must double and triple our efforts and do it 24/7. We don't have many opportunities, so we shouldn't complain or lament. We must simply work. The sales department should sell day and night, and the production department must work 24/7. With that spirit, the entire company worked tirelessly. At that time, selling was still easy. Thanks to our excellent reputation in the coffee, peppercorn and spice industries and the coconut and cashew nut industries, we sold and exported day and night.

As expected, the epidemic became a pandemic, and the global situation became more difficult. Europe and the US entered lockdown. By the end of April, our exports increased by 14 percent over the same period last year. Coffee, peppercorn, and other items all sold well above what was expected. Looking back on what I did at the end of the year, I see it was a moment of very wise decision-making.

However, deciding to produce and sell goods day and night domestically required that I cancel all trips abroad. First, Dubai, then India, Africa, Europe, and America. Many people went to Dubai in February, but I thought it would be safer for the company's management team and me to cancel the trip, even if they didn't return the money. I thought people were more important. However, if I didn't go abroad to attend fairs and seminars and visit customers, what should I do instead?

I suddenly remembered that almost all my friends, acquaintances and partners always ask, "Phuc Sinh exports so much; where can we buy such innovative products?" That question returned when difficulties piled up. Countries under lockdown didn't buy any goods. Moreover, sold contracts could still be shipped after February, but it would be difficult to buy new items. It was easy to convince the customer before, but now it was much more difficult. I had to find the right market. But under lockdown, how to buy and sell was a big question. So an idea came up: Should I drastically attack the domestic market? If one can't go abroad, one must try the domestic market. So the entire company eagerly dove into the domestic market, designing quality products, upgrading the packaging and finishing online purchasing avenues.

We had a lot of things before that were unfinished. We finished them to perfection and created more. We did a lot of things. We introduced new products, like freeze-dried green peppercorn, peppercorn sauce, cascara tea, pink peppercorn and four-season peppercorn. We worked as we had never worked before. While the market was quiet, people asked why Phuc Sinh worked so much. I just replied that I couldn't go abroad this year, so I just pivoted and focused on doing well domestically.

At the same time, we were looking for ways to improve the online site. We wanted to figure out how to sell to customers without them having to go to the market to shop during the pandemic. Finally, we also perfected and continuously upgraded our shopping app called KPhucSinh. People always asked how it was possible to do so much and commented that it must have cost a lot of money. Our answer was very simple. We had invested in IT software for 15 years, so the app was just the visible part of the system. The pressing question was that the cost of selling online must be a lot of money, right? The answer was that we had invested like this for a long time, both through direct investment and a cost-sharing system, so running and managing online was really not too much. Some plans often used to be dreams on paper, but it was time to speed them up to success.

I went to Europe to visit a top customer there. After eating, they invited us to drink coffee. They printed my picture on the coffee cup! I looked at it in amazement, hoping to bring that technology back to Vietnam. After years of talking and this year's push, we finally have that printer in our shop. Needless to say, people were so happy to be drinking a cappuccino cup with their picture on it, and many people came to the shop to try it. Thanks to that, the shop sold a lot. Customers also bought plenty of our coffee and peppercorn products.

Phuc Sinh has an enormous advantage; it is a very reputable company. Most suppliers give credit to Phuc Sinh, and Phuc Sinh can offer very good discounts to its customers.

In May, the world improved, and summer brought many emotions for everyone. Countries also lifted their restrictions. However, it seemed that customers could buy goods again, but the goods they had stocked up on from January to April 2020 were still plentiful. Many people lamented they bought too much. Now warehouses were still intact but almost motionless. What to do? We often concentrated on small and medium private companies worldwide, but these companies encountered great difficulties. The demand doubled for big companies that specialized in providing large supermarkets or online markets. We tried to find a better approach; we had a relationship with them before. Phuc Sinh's excellent reputation also helped a lot. We had to turn to focus entirely on this customer segment. Things seemed a little better, but a month later, this customer segment also had difficulty. They requested to delay the delivery dates, and even big customers asked to move to next year. It was impossible to describe such challenges.

However, when looking at the whole, we had an international customer base. It must be said that they were great; the customers we had chosen over the years carried the motto of kindness, respect for different cultures and healthy finances. This saved us many difficult years and allowed us to overcome many challenges. However, Covid-19 did not spare anyone. Many of our customers had been in business for nearly 20 years, 10 years and 15 years. They were all older than me. I worried about them and prayed for their health and families to overcome this pandemic.

Domestic work was also difficult. Sometimes at 4 or 5 a.m., we had to rush to the market or go to the street to sell goods. When you receive an order from a foreign customer, and they confirm it, it would be considered having been placed and closed. But receiving a domestic order is just the beginning, and it is not certain that you can sell the goods. Some people assure us they will buy dozens of boxes of goods, then simply disappear or apologize. Management can also say that the contract is about to be signed, ordering billions of dollars worth of goods to be produced, but then there is no contract! They consider it very normal. Build a grand plan to spend money and then cancel, taking no responsibility at all. This is far different from the exporting business. What can be done? You can only re-adjust yourself.

It is a very good thing that we have been exporting and trading with the world for many years; now it is very convenient. That is the professional way of thinking and doing things. You build factory systems and standards for importers in the world's advanced countries. Back in Vietnam, I excelled. You create sustainable development and make a deed with developed countries. Then you come back to Vietnam to see many businesses that only invested at the top, even very large companies in the industry. They only focus on the boss or the General Director, who is also the boss. Contrarily, we build utilities for management staff and invest a lot for everyone in Phuc Sinh. Customers, partners, and friends come to our office and say, "Why does only Phuc Sinh create such benefits for their employees?" For me, it is not the customers who are the gods, but the employees by my side who are the gods of the company! This inspires us all a lot.

For sales, we must attend many conferences and programs and meet many local companies. We share sincerely, and they like it very much. We are much more valuable when sharing about the system and management, so we are busy sharing. This helps us improve and helps us to sell more. After all that, we feel very fortunate. After many years of competing with leading companies in our industry in the world, returning to our home country is a significant advantage. However, I really see that Vietnamese businesses have not focused on investing in advanced software systems. If the world further develops information technology and digitization at such rapid speeds, we will have a big setback. Because I always find myself falling behind, I strive for continuous improvement whenever possible. Someone asked me, "When the number conversion is completed, will it be over then?" The answer is that it is just the beginning and shall never end!

Returning to the export business, because of Covid, peppercorn prices have dropped to the lowest levels in the past 10 years. Buyers and sellers have congested connections. Doing business is difficult. When the price goes down, the buyers in many markets would think the price will drop even lower and stop buying. When the price rises, customers think it will continue increasing, so they all order simultaneously. That's what happens. When the price goes down, it's hard to sell, but it's easy to sell when it goes up. At the same time, one of our longtime customers wanted to cancel their contract. This customer had been established for nearly 20 years in one of the most prestigious markets in the world. The price at the time they bought was high, but the price when we delivered was low, and the customer wanted to cancel.

The trader was quite worried. I told her she should convince the customer not to cancel. Their name was very important, and the trader tried to convince them, but the customer still canceled the contract with the excuse of quality. Then it was my turn to convince. They, the buyer, were very arrogant, and in the end I said if they didn't want to do it, I would take it to the London Arbitration Center (LAC). They never thought a Vietnamese company in this difficult time would dare do so. But we said we were out of options. We tried to reach an agreement, but they didn't listen, so we took it to the LAC. We sued them, and they were shocked. We thought that after many years of doing business worldwide, everyone in the industry knew Phuc Sinh's name. How could we confidently continue to do business if we couldn't do this? We had no other option if they insisted on canceling. We gave them a deadline, but they didn't change their minds, so we turned in the documents and paid a huge sum of money, not to mention that it was in pounds sterling. After many explanations, we finally won and got a clear verdict. The whole European market, all the buyers, supported us. In fact, there are always these different people in business, but it is not a reason to make you lose faith in life.

But in general, Europeans respect contracts and business agreements, so it is one of the safest markets in the world. One morning when we went to the office, the finance department informed me we had just received a large amount of money in the account. We carefully checked and found that it was consistent with the verdict of the LAC, which concluded that the sued business was required to pay Phuc Sinh. We were very happy. First, we recovered the full amount we paid upfront to the LAC, and second, we received all the arbitration money while gaining stronger confidence in the global market. The situation in the world is still getting more and more difficult. Covid-19 still impacts all continents. Travel is banned, and we can never be sure when the lockdown will end. Every day, we meet with the sales department for ten minutes to coordinate customer care, always encouraging each other to make more sales. Otherwise, we will not overcome this challenge.

On the other hand, domestic business is hard. People may initially be happy with certain goods but eventually lose interest. There must continuously be new and good-quality products. During the Mid-Autumn Festival, we released many items, such as the Box of Happiness and four seasons peppercorn, which are peppercorn products that were presented to the Vietnamese market for the first time. Of course, we had black peppercorn and white peppercorn, but for the first time, there was natural green peppercorn, both freeze-dried and dried, and pink peppercorn: beautiful, very delicious and refreshing. Then the Happy Box was beautifully designed, like a work of art. All of that resulted from the company's constant effort to introduce good products to Vietnamese consumers. Above all, through creativity, we find a way to overcome difficulties.

When we created the KPhucSinh app, we thought that since we made it convenient for customers to buy and sell online anyway, why don't we just sell everything at once? Isn't it more convenient for customers and also more profitable? So we contacted our suppliers, and many responded with a great spirit of cooperation. Now we sell many products on the KPhucSinh app, and the revenue is constantly increasing. We know that we have to continuously improve the app system so that it runs quickly, smoothly and conveniently and offers good prices so that customers who have purchased in the past will always return to support us.

This year has not ended, and we remain hopeful. We still hope that the coffee crop expected from October to February next year and the peppercorn crop from late November and December onwards will bring many goods. We will try to export a lot to earn more money. However, shipping lines have changed their game rules. They do not allow sending ships in with empty containers. Freight rates have increased by five to seven times and have stopped all business connections. It is extremely difficult to get empty containers, so there is no way to export the goods. On top of those challenges, the shipping companies canceled all orders for low-priced containers, creating a chaotic market. We have reduced our export volume by 75 percent over the same period.

In the winter, there was a strong re-emergence of Covid-19. Thousands of people died daily in the US, South America, Europe and many other places worldwide. Europe and the US entered their second lockdown period. At that time, I found the world very dark. What could I do? I knew there was always a way out; maybe I just hadn't found it in this instance. If I tried, I would find a way.

At the end of the year, we sold many goods in the domestic market. Everyone enthusiastically supported K Coffee and K Peppercorn as well as the KPhucSinh app. Our sales increased tremendously in every way. Sometimes everyone had to go selling goods at 4 a.m.; sometimes we had to convince customers, and sometimes it was friends and partners who supported us. Some customers have a lot of love for K Coffee. Such great support helped Phuc Sinh Consumer Corporation to be profitable for the first time during its four years of establishment.

Thanks to customers worldwide in over 100 countries, we have always been supported during the past year. They have continuously expressed their trust in Phuc Sinh, so we overcame all the difficult and dangerous challenges.

I wish the world peace and health as we enter 2021. I hope everyone, every family, has enough money in their account so that no one goes hungry. I hope this pandemic ends so that the world can return to normal, so we can continue having jobs. I wish for our buyers to be able to sell, for our partners to be healthy, and for us to have business orders. I desire for everyone to overcome difficulties and grow!

Ho Chi Minh City, January 2, 2021.

AUTHENTIC CEOS

The phone rang. "Hello, Thien. This is Minh. I am sitting with Mr. Quang, the owner of a large company, K Coffee. They need a CEO to run the company. Thien, send your info to K Coffee."

"That's great," said Thien. "Let me send my CV immediately."

The next day, Thien had a conversation with Linh, the Human Resources Director of K Coffee.

"I've looked at the supermarket system. The product design is very nice. I have tried the coffee. It is good, but the product is a bit limited on display. The salary needs to be favorable, then I'll do it," Thien told Linh.

"God, why are you demanding such a high wage?"

"As you know, I was CEO of many companies and worked for a big company, MZ Group. The previous company also paid me a high salary. If it's lower, I can't do it."

"Let me talk to the Board of Directors; then I'll talk to you again," Linh replied.

Two days later, the contract was negotiated. It was the first meeting with the owner of the company.

"Mr. Quang, rest assured that I will build a detailed KPI and never fail that number. I always exceed KPIs," Thien said.

"Yeah, do your best. There have been many people in the past who were all bark, no bite. They said grand things but did nothing. Then the company has had to go pick up all that garbage, time and time again."

"Don't worry," Thien said. "I do what I say, and I do it fiercely."

Thien sent Quang and his team the entire plan and KPI a week later. Revenue was forecast to be 80 billion VND, and the starting salary was already 30 billion VND. "I'll start with this number. It's not big, but it's realistic. I will build from scratch."

"Why does it cost so much?"

"Yes, it has to cost that much in order to create revenue."

"Try your best. Many people have made promises and taken money from the company, so now the management is very wary."

"You can rest assured," Thien replied.

The next week:

"I must say that the company looks beautiful and majestic on the outside, but inside, it feels broken and in debt. Everything is cluttered. Linh, why is there such debt and so many returned goods?" Thien asked.

"We need to rearrange and address all of that. We needed to hire you," Linh replied

"I've checked the accounting books. The company owes its suppliers. Especially the one running the sampling program, that's SkyLine."

"Yes, the former CEO made the program. He promised the company's leadership that it would have a revenue of 2.3 billion VND. He spent 1.6 billion VND. He bought many things back home: speakers, cabinets, audio equipment ... all kinds of things, but now everything is just junk. Conniving to get money from the company, spent 1.6 billion VND to get 600 million VND. Our company is reviewing the record to see if it is correct. Sampling goods have been returned in abundance, and the devices are all broken," Linh said.

"Block the payment to the old CEO. Let me call him back," Thien said.

"Yes, I will do it right away."

The chief accountant told Thien, "SkyLine has been calling all day to collect a debt. Please, give me the payment schedule."

"Try to convince them that the company will pay slowly. I am doing my best," Thien replied.

"I negotiated a high salary and earned the owner's trust, but I also have to try. I don't have many relationships and am not good at sales either. I do not know what to do ..." Thien mourned to himself.

He just thought that looking at the grandeur of the company and the beautiful products, the sales must be good, with good network coverage. But that was just on the outside. The revenue was really not good. His old company sold cosmetics. He had no associations whatsoever with coffee, peppercorn or FMCG goods. Too hard!

"What should I do? Now there must be sales, but sales are too difficult. The employees are lazy, only fake working, doing light work but asking for high wages; I have to tighten it. How to make sales here? This month's goal is 4 billion VND, which is not a small number at all …" A thought flashed: "Should I ask my relatives and acquaintances to make contracts and then transfer money to the company, then I will continue selling it to them? If they are unable to sell, they can return the goods to the company and get their money back. But I have to exceed this month's KPI first. Too difficult. Just have to do that. I will think of what to do next later …"

"Mr. Quang, I heard the staff say that Mr. Thien lamented a lot, saying that the company only has the cover but no network, and owes SkyLine. He is saying that he wouldn't have accepted the job if he knew this," Linh shared.

"Yes, we want to develop. That's why we hired a new CEO. We are even paying such a high salary for good products and a good company name if we are able. And with the industry relationships he said he had, why couldn't he do it?"

"Yes, I think that too. I'm just sharing information," Linh said.

At the meeting at the end of the month:

"Why is the revenue so low? Sales are 800 million VND, but your salary is already 220 million VND. Not to mention paying another 40 employees …"

"I tried my best."

"So, where are the things you promised when you got the job? Where? The KPI is 4 billion VND, but you only reached 800 million VND."

There was just silence …

"Please give me five more days to try this month."

"Okay, do your best."

The Chief Accountant, named Truong, called Mr. Quang. "The company has run out of money to pay suppliers and salaries."

"Why don't you call Thien?"

"Mr. Thien can't help with anything."

"Okay, let me transfer the money."

During the following months, Mr. Quang always received calls from the Chief Accountant.

"Mr. Quang, I …"

"Come on! Just go over there and tell Mr. Thien that receiving a terrific salary means he must take the initiative to do business! Why just keep asking for money?" Quang said.

"Yes, I know, but I don't know where to get the money when I must pay the salaries and the supplier," Truong said.

A new month coming with high targeted sales revenue made Thien think, "I shall use the same trick again." He discussed it with the manager of the company.

"Hai, tell the dealers and supermarkets we will give them a big discount and then make an agency contract. If they cannot sell, we will change the products with new expiry dates for them or return the money. Do it with all the dealers," Thien said.

"Have you submitted this plan to the Board of Directors?" Hai asked.

"Just do it; we must make the sales. Try to get the dealers to sell, and you should also try to sell. Try to achieve the target."

"If they can't sell in the end, and they want to change the products with a new expiry date or return the goods, what should we do?" Hai continued to ask.

"Then we will think later; we must achieve the KPI, must get the salary first."

Four months later, the goods shipped to the company piled up and could not be sold. Dealers kept calling to ask for money. Too many near-date goods were returned; even our large warehouse had no space to store them.

"Thien, why have the dealers returned so much? They even called me on my phone, always asking for money and cursing so much. They said we are ignoring them and not being reputable as promised," Linh said.

"Let me think; I'll talk to the dealers," Thien replied.

During the next eight months, the situation had not improved. The goods returned from the dealers which filled the warehouse from the first to the sixth floor were all close to or out of date.

"I probably can't continue to work here; the returned goods are all close to and out of date. There's no way back. Relatives, acquaintances and dealers, I've used them all; now what? I should probably quit the job, but the pay is so good! What a pity! I should look for another job ..." Thien thought to himself.

"Mr. Quang, shouldn't you have handled it by now? I see Thien doesn't know how to run anything. He just knows people who can make the packaging beautiful. Returned goods cannot be sold; the company still has to pay wages and loses too much money. And there's one thing I feel obliged to tell you: The dealers called me one day, and they asked why we're not paying them. They said we have no credibility," Linh said.

"Is that so? Maybe you have to talk to Thien. We must take things more seriously; otherwise, this has to end."

"Yes!"

"But I find myself hiring too many CEOs that all fail; maybe I was not thorough and drastic enough in each evaluation. They're all fake; the returns are piling up like a mountain; they are a bunch of scammers!" Quang said.

The company was in such a terrible state, with no strategy and revenue being far too low. Thien mourned, "But I have to get enough of the salary before I quit my job. Today I will give the resignation letter to Linh."

"Mr. Quang, Mr. Thien sent me this." Linh panicked and sent him Thien's resignation letter.

"Does he have a plan to handle the returns? He's the executive CEO, but he's doing it wrong. Promising a KPI that he cannot achieve, not even handling the close-to-date goods that customers returned, causing a tremendous loss. Has he no responsibility at all, no conscience at all?" Quang said.

"I shall withhold his salary," Linh replied.

"Withhold it, and I will talk to Thien to see if he is taking any responsibility."

The next week, payday:

"Linh, where's my salary? Didn't I sign the payroll before leaving the company?" Thien asked.

"Mr. Thien, you need to hand over the work and be responsible for handling the short-date goods and the company's losses. You didn't process anything, and now the goods have all become out-of-date and must be disposed of, making the company lose billions."

"Aren't you going to pay me? Isn't the company going to pay me? I'll leak this news to the press. You and the company will take it hard!"

The following week:

"Are you Quang? I'm with TCX Newspaper. Your business is KM Coffee Company, right? Mr. Thien said that you did not pay his salary. I want to interview you."

"Hi, I'm too busy, and the company is also suing Thien. He caused us to lose property and is irresponsible. His actions led to a great deal of damage and huge monetary losses. The company is preparing for a lawsuit. I will reply when I have more details!"

Two days later:

"Mr. Quang, our company is already in the press, and there are pictures of you too."

"What's the matter?"

"The case involving Thien. He hired the press to write nonsense about our company."

"Okay, calm down. We didn't do anything. No need to be afraid," Quang replied.

"But the press is really hungry for news. They haven't verified anything, yet the company's image and yours are already sullied," Linh said. "I also heard that Thien and Mr. Hung, the chief representative of this newspaper, used to work together at the VifasAcecok noodle company in the past and had an old business relationship."

The next day:

"Hello, Linh. Are you happy?" Thien said, "Will the company pay me my salary now?"

"Thien, you really don't have any dignity or self-respect. The company is looking into a salary settlement and looking to hold you accountable for billions of lost and destroyed goods. Your employees have worked with you for almost a year, but now this is how you treat the company and them? Were you the CEO? The company is going to sue you; we will file a lawsuit this afternoon. Just accept it," Linh said.

"So go ahead and sue. I have nothing to fear!"

"There's nothing wrong with me; I have to receive a salary for my work," Thien said to himself. "The company had no profit and was already losing money. I did what I could. I didn't do anything wrong. What could I do when so many goods were returned? And the KPI was too big, but I found a way to achieve it that time. But? I tried to sell to relatives and friends to boost sales. At that time, I thought I should just sell it because the contract included the right to return, but I also thought of selling it first and then looking for a way to deal with them. Who would have thought that one month would pass so quickly? It just continued endlessly. Never mind, I already left. Now I must look for a way to get that salary. Everything else later. Now to go find a new job!"

The case dragged on for many years.

"Linh, I'm so tired. You know I'm not wrong, right?" Thien called Linh.

"You know it's your responsibility, but no one would dare hire a CEO like you. Shifty and irresponsible. In my opinion, if you want the company to stop suing, then pay the company."

"But you see, I didn't make any mistakes ..."

"Then keep pursuing this case; whoever hires you will see the company's lawsuit regarding your irresponsible behavior, and people will probably faint." Linh hung up.

"Hey, I'm talking! My head hurts so much I don't know when this will be over ..."

Covid, lockdown days, September 22, 2021.

LOVE OF ARTS

Today, Trang went to a party organized by a friend and discovered a big collector at the party named Minh. Trang had heard a lot about this person and tried to reach out to him many times, but it was difficult. She saw him at today's party.

"Hi, Mr. Minh. I'm Trang. I specialize in brokering beautiful and precious paintings. I'm an artist as well. I've heard about you for a long time; everyone keeps talking about you. It's nice to finally meet you today."

"Hi, Ms. Trang. It's nice to meet you. Mr. Dung did a great job today with this event; everyone can finally meet."

"Yes, this is the only way to cross paths with you! Minh, my mother has a beautiful gallery. She's been working in the industry for a long time. Come to see it someday."

"Alright, give me the address; I'll come to see it someday."
"By the way, let's exchange phone numbers."

Life goes by. Weeks later:

"Mr. Minh, how are you? Why is it so hard to contact you?"
"I'm sorry, I keep having to go on business trips."
"When can you come to the gallery to see it?"
"Let me see. I'm too busy these days."

Two months later, Minh went to visit his friend's house, who is also the owner of a famous gallery in Saigon.

"Oh, what a beautiful painting, Tam. Is it Do Xuan Doan's?"
"Yes, that's right, Mr. Minh. These were painted by Do Xuan Doan."

"How could you have so many beautiful paintings by Do Xuan Doan!"

"I own the gallery, Mr. Minh!"

"It is true that Do Xuan Doan's paintings are really beautiful. The more I see them, the more beautiful they become. Mr. Doan's lacquer paintings are so amazing! They must be very expensive," Minh thought to himself. "I have collected many artists' paintings, but there are very few paintings by Do Xuan Doan. Maybe I will buy one when I have the opportunity," Minh said to himself.

Many months later, Ms. Trang called again.

"Mr. Minh, come to visit my mother's gallery. She has a large set of paintings by Do Xuan Doan. They were collected by a French client in Vietnam 20 years ago. So beautiful."

"Do Xuan Doan? I will come right away."

Ten minutes later, Minh was in Trang's mother's gallery. After a few minutes of introduction, Minh was led to the third floor to see 40 paintings by Do Xuan Doan. It must be said that they were very beautiful. Mrs. Nga, Trang's mother, said that Francois, a Frenchman, had collected through her for the past 20 years and was now returning to France, so he wanted to sell this collection. Mrs. Nga showed Minh many valuable and historical documents from decades ago and her business relationship with Mr. Do Xuan Doan. After two weeks of consultation, Minh bought almost all the Frenchman's Do Xuan Doan collection.

Minh paid in three installments. After he paid the second installment, Mrs. Nga sent someone to hang all the paintings from the gallery in Minh's house. The paintings were so sparkling and beautiful that when Minh posted the first few paintings on Facebook, many people shared and commented.

The next day, Minh received a call from Trang's colleague in the industry.

"I also have some beautiful paintings of Do Xuan Doan; do you want to buy them?"

"Yes, let me see."

Once again, after a period of negotiation, Minh bought a very beautiful painting of a Vietnamese girl.

When receiving the painting, Minh let them hang it up. He took a photo of it and shared it on Facebook, titled *Glittering by Do Xuan Doan*. Minh's post was shared and commented on by many people. But things weren't what they seemed ...

"You should probably take a closer look. Are those Do Xuan Doan's paintings?" Out of nowhere, someone entered a comment and claimed to be an artist.

"Dear Mr. Minh, this is a painting by the young artist Do Hung. Be careful; you may have bought fake paintings," a Facebook friend sent to Minh.

"I don't think it's a fake because my friend was also the owner of the gallery and had a photo together with Mr. Do Xuan Doan," Minh replied.

Though it was quiet, the trouble had just begun. The next day, Minh woke up, and after breakfast, he looked at Facebook and jumped up. Hundreds of hostile and disparaging messages. Someone pretended to be a journalist in order to share and criticize. A friend copied it and sent it to Minh. Minh was a bit surprised. How was this possible?

Minh was a little confused and surprised when he received a phone call from a journalist friend.

"Mr. Minh, I just went to your Facebook and saw how they jumped in the comments, cursing and disparaging the painting you posted on Facebook. I think it's beautiful. Why would they say that? Many people claim to be the painter's friend; why would young artists speak like they know nothing? I read but couldn't understand ..."

"I don't know either," Minh replied. "I bought Do Xuan Doan's painting from my friend. I got a certificate and a photo of Uncle Doan with the painting, but someone said it looks like Do Hung paintings on silk."

"Oh yeah. Well, maybe he copied the young artist's painting. But I see, through his hand, the painting became much more beautiful. There is more depth and artistry. It's just that he drew on a topic that inspired other people a long time ago. But I see people commenting who don't understand the painting and think they're experts. This is the original painting, not a fake. It's just that he drew a theme that other people employed a long time ago," his friend replied.

"Yes, I see that the paintings of famous Vietnamese artists also imitate foreign painters a lot, from color matching to simply learning from their thinking. When I visit museums in Europe and America, I see many paintings from 300 years ago. Back in Vietnam, famous painters also painted very closely to that style. Moreover, artists of Indochina painted in exactly the same way! How can they draw thousands of paintings in such a short time?"

"I heard they were painters in France, not our Indochinese painters. They copy paintings of our own artists. There are copy-painting studios all over the world! Looking at the painters in Montmartre Hill, I think their work is more beautiful than that of our professional painters. For our people, most things would just follow the trends. Buying paintings is also a trend! And in my opinion, if painter Do Xuan Doan paints a painting with a young artist's theme, then I think the young artist should be proud. If a famous painter paints according to his theme, he should be very honored," the journalist said.

Maybe paintings like this are beautiful, but the value will not be as high compared to the original creation in both ideas and drawings. However, seeing so much controversy, Minh decided not to hang it anymore. He was afraid of the way young artists thought in this case. They jumped in and cursed a lot, all claiming to be painters and knowledgeable. However, he didn't sell anything; he bought it himself because it was created by artist Do Xuan Doan, who maybe only painted on order. Through this, he also saw pettiness and was afraid of such an extreme reaction. People were so rude, and they cursed a lot. He wouldn't have believed it if he hadn't experienced it for himself.

"Yes, social media is like that now. They just play the mob, but it's all in the name of art and love. So be careful," said his friend.

"Yes, thank you."

The following week, Mrs. Nga called Minh. Maybe it was because Trang told her, she couldn't sleep when she heard the entire story, and the Frenchman was also angry.

"Don't worry; I'll be fine. I know what's right and what's wrong. What's real and what's fake! With your prestige and all the information, I believe I know the right paintings of Mr. Do Xuan Doan. Mr. Doan is a great painter of Vietnam. This painting of the girl is also his painting, but it's probably one he made on order. And looking at his history, I think it's normal." Minh said to Mrs. Nga.

"Yes, if you say that, then I can rest assured. Don't let those uneducated talkers affect you," said Mrs. Nga.

"Yes, that's social media. People say whatever they want and say it to their heart's content, but if they had thought about it, they wouldn't say that. As a collector, I know beauty, aesthetic orientation, and how to preserve the real and the fake, ma'am, rest assured."

Two weeks after the due date, Minh went to the gallery to pay the rest of the money to Mrs. Nga.

"Over 30 years in the art business, I have never seen anyone with the same heart and reputation as you. Everyone says you are number one, and, through this turbulent time, I see that you really are."

"Thank you," Minh replied.

Minh walked out of the gallery and went back to the office. The sky was clear but windy.

Covid during lockdown days, September 27, 2021.

Rate this book on our website!

www.novum-publishing.co.uk

The author

Phan Minh Thong is the founder and CEO of Phuc Sinh Corporation; the number one company in Vietnam in pepper importing-exporting and one of the top five largest companies in the country for exporting coffee. As of 2016, Phuc Sinh's export sales reached US$300 million.

He has been leading Phuc Sinh Corporation since 2001 and has many achievements to his name: The title of prestigious Exporter of the Ministry of Industry and Trade; Certified in the ranking of the 500 largest private enterprises in Vietnam; Certificate of Merit from the Minister of Agriculture and Rural Development, being just a few. In 2016, he was honored by being named 'Typical Businessman in Vietnam.'

This story came to him in a dream many years ago and has stuck in his head ever since. It was a story he just felt compelled to write! While on his business travels, he would write about his experiences. Overcoming Business Journeys is an expansion of those notes.

novum PUBLISHER FOR NEW AUTHORS

The publisher

*He who stops
getting better
stops being good.*

This is the motto of novum publishing, and our focus is on finding new manuscripts, publishing them and offering long-term support to the authors.
Our publishing house was founded in 1997, and since then it has become THE expert for new authors and has won numerous awards.

Our editorial team will peruse each manuscript within a few weeks free of charge and without obligation.

You will find more information about
novum publishing and our books on the internet:

w w w . n o v u m - p u b l i s h i n g . c o . u k

www.ingramcontent.com/pod-product-compliance
Lightning Source LLC
LaVergne TN
LVHW020912061025
822564LV00042B/175